Donald Trump in the Frontier Mythology

This book explores the presidential image of Donald Trump as it is constructed by the media within American national mythology, precisely the frontier myth.

By offering an account of three milestones in the development of the frontier mythology in its intersection with presidential imagery, the book shows how the image of Donald Trump fits into the line of "cowboy presidents," together with Theodore Roosevelt and Ronald Reagan. It also offers insights into the reasons for making Russian president Vladimir Putin a part of Trump's story and a routinely mentioned figure in American presidential politics.

Applying the means of philosophical anthropology to this topical issue at the intersection of politics and the media, this volume will appeal to those working and studying in the areas of media studies, political anthropology, American studies, and myth studies.

Olena Leipnik is Lecturer in the Department of Sociology at Sam Houston State University, USA.

Routledge Studies in Media, Communication, and Politics

10. **White Supremacy and the American Media**
    Edited By Sarah D. Nilsen, Sarah E. Turner

11. **Tweeting Brexit**
    Social Media and the Aftermath of the EU Referendum
    Maja Šimunjak

12. **Knowledge Resistance in High-Choice Information Environments**
    Edited By Jesper Strömbäck, Åsa Wikforss, Kathrin Glüer, Torun Lindholm, Henrik Oscarsson

13. **A Media Framing Approach to Securitization**
    Storytelling in Conflict, Crisis and Threat
    Fred Vultee

14. **Gender Violence, Social Media, and Online Environments**
    When the Virtual Becomes Real
    Lisa M. Cuklanz

15. **Right-Wing Media's Neurocognitive and Societal Effects**
    Rodolfo Levya

16. **The Economic Policy of Online Media**
    Manufacture of Dissent
    Peter Ayolov

17. **Donald Trump in the Frontier Mythology**
    Olena Leipnik

www.routledge.com/Routledge-Studies-in-Media-Communication-and-Politics/book-series/RSMCP

Donald Trump in the Frontier Mythology

Olena Leipnik

LONDON AND NEW YORK

First published 2023
by Routledge
4 Park Square, Milton Park, Abingdon, Oxon OX14 4RN

and by Routledge
605 Third Avenue, New York, NY 10158

Routledge is an imprint of the Taylor & Francis Group, an informa business

© 2023 Olena Leipnik

The right of Olena Leipnik to be identified as author of this work has been asserted in accordance with sections 77 and 78 of the Copyright, Designs and Patents Act 1988.

All rights reserved. No part of this book may be reprinted or reproduced or utilised in any form or by any electronic, mechanical, or other means, now known or hereafter invented, including photocopying and recording, or in any information storage or retrieval system, without permission in writing from the publishers.

Trademark notice: Product or corporate names may be trademarks or registered trademarks, and are used only for identification and explanation without intent to infringe.

British Library Cataloguing-in-Publication Data
A catalogue record for this book is available from the British Library

Library of Congress Cataloging-in-Publication Data
Names: Leipnik, Olena V., author.
Title: Donald Trump in the frontier mythology/Olena Leipnik.
Description: Abingdon, Oxon; New York: Routledge, 2023. |
  Series: Routledge studies in media, communication, and politics |
  Includes bibliographical references and index.
Identifiers: LCCN 2023009831 (print) | LCCN 2023009832 (ebook) |
  ISBN 9781032541310 (hardback) | ISBN 9781032541327 (paperback) |
  ISBN 9781003415312 (ebook)
Subjects: LCSH: Trump, Donald, 1946– | Myth-Political aspects—United
  States. | Frontier thesis. | Toughness (Personality trait) | Political
  culture—United States—History—21st century.
Classification: LCC E912 .L428 2023 (print) | LCC E912 (ebook) |
  DDC 973.933092—dc23/eng/20230315
LC record available at https://lccn.loc.gov/2023009831
LC ebook record available at https://lccn.loc.gov/2023009832

ISBN: 978-1-032-54131-0 (hbk)
ISBN: 978-1-032-54132-7 (pbk)
ISBN: 978-1-003-41531-2 (ebk)

DOI: 10.4324/9781003415312

Typeset in Times New Roman
by Apex CoVantage, LLC

Contents

	Preface	*vii*
1	**"The toughest guy in the office"**	1
	The tough guy theme in politics 1	
	Masculine politics and the origin of the tough 5	
2	**Theodore Roosevelt: the becoming of the frontier and the arrival of the hero**	11
	Performative frontier: staging the myth 11	
	The enduring contradiction of myth 16	
	The land and the man 20	
	The man and the towners 26	
	The girl: gendered opposition 30	
3	**Ronald Reagan: extension of the frontier and inversion of the hero**	35
	Myth gains primacy 35	
	The exhauster of myth 38	
4	**Donald Trump: recovered meanings of the frontier and resurgence of the hero**	46
	Back to the beginning 46	
	New scapes: cowboy goes metropolitan 51	
	Myth continued 54	

5 Vladimir Putin: "stolen" meanings of the frontier and a supplementing hero   57
Here comes the villain 57
"Is he one of us?" 58

Concluding thoughts   61

Index   65

Preface

The way a story of a politician is told makes the difference on election day. The political image of Donald Trump has been fashioned to fit his unconventional character into the POTUS gallery—the gallery of men (for now, only men) expected to possess outstanding personal and professional qualities, the all-national heroes, embodiments of the national character, whatever the latter means. By the end of Trump's term in office, his conflict with the mainstream media reached the point where the media blocked him from public presence; for many years before that, however, the media, both entertainment and news, were shaping his image to, eventually, click with the voters and help him into office. Whether Trump won 2016 election primarily because of media impact or because he was a self-made success, it was not an actual creator of the image, but the content and the meanings the image had capitalized on that mattered.

This book was inspired by two observations. The first observation was that some traits of Trump's image, not the most conventional for a presidential candidate, were overly emphasized by the commentators and himself, and despite their controversial character connected him well with the electorate. The second observation was that, as a presidential candidate, Trump seemed to be immune to the consequences of some of his statements, actions, and elements of his bio that could, normally, sink a political reputation.

The inquiry presented here is based on an assumption that a successful political image incorporates those mostly unarticulated mental patterns that underlie the "likes" and "dislikes" of the audiences more than overt ideological stances, that if a bond between a politician as a media persona and the audience escapes rational explanations, it must have been formed at a deeper level than that of ideology and defined by a different kind of rationale—it is defined by the logic of myth.

Building upon the literature on American frontier mythology, the book lays out two major theses. First, the storytelling about Donald Trump intended for the public and delivered through the mass media posits his presidential image, intentionally or unintentionally, against the American national mythology, precisely the myth of the Western frontier. Second, the image of Trump incorporated into the frontier mythology would be incomplete without a supporting character, in which role stars the president of the Russian Federation, Vladimir Putin. Regardless of what the relations between the two men really are and whether "the Russian collusion" had at all happened, Putin emerged in Trump's story by his side as a necessary element of the continuation of the frontier saga.

The discussion around each of the two names has always been highly politicized, and it has become overheated to the extreme in the last years. Yet, this volume is intended not to present a stand in a political debate but, on the contrary, approach the subject academically. Staying within the conceptual framework of myth studies, it implies the dialectical approach, showing the forming of a new essence through the inner contradiction, in this case the formation of American national consciousness as the basis for national unity, for the everlasting process of the formation of the nation. The nation-formative myth is scrutinized on its inner logic and the elements built into its content, the features that ensured the functioning of the myth as a factor in politics, the development of the myth through major milestones, and the modifications that prolonged its life after its inner logic had been exhausted.

This volume is a version of what was initially planned as a chapter in a manuscript titled "Trump and Putin in Media Mythologies." It had to be developed into a separate piece, though, because tracking the development of the major American national myth in its relation to presidential imagery caused the research to deviate from the initial format and objectives. The manuscript "Trump and Putin in Media Mythologies" partly builds upon the findings presented in the current volume and covers the following themes: mythologization and archetypal meanings of presidential imagery; spatial and temporal characteristics of American and Russian cultures as they are presented in presidential imagery or Donald Trump and Vladimir Putin; and myth (for American culture) and fairy tale (for Russian culture) as two ways of telling a presidential story.

1 "The toughest guy in the office"

The tough guy theme in politics

The tough guy rhetoric became a dominating theme in constructing Trump's presidential image through both self-reporting and depiction in the media. "The GOP's Tough Guy"—the title of a Rolling Stone article about Trump (Solotaroff 2015)—described how he self-reported his toughness in many ways before and after securing the presidency. "I am the toughest guy in the office," he announced when, after his meeting with Putin at the NATO Summit, he was criticized for not opposing Putin's toughness in the same—tough—manner. "We have to get tough so that our country can be great again"; "I would be so tough you would not believe"; "I would handle it so tough, you don't want to hear"; "We are going to handle it so tough"; "It's a big job to handle, and one has to prove they are 'tough enough for the job'"—one could go on and on citing Trump's statements on his own exceptional toughness. The reputation of "the tough" had been made into a core feature of Trump's character before he disclosed his presidential ambitions; his book published in 2011 was titled "Time to Get Tough: Making America #1 Again," and it was a trait, he claimed, passed down to him: "My father was a terrific guy. Wonderful man. Tough guy. Very tough," praised Trump his father in 2013 interview with David Letterman (AmericanShow 2013). Toughness in negotiation, toughness in sorting out the job seekers, tough grasp of doing business.

At that, the image of the tough was more important than actual toughness. Back in the 1980s, in one of his interviews, Trump reacted to the media portraying him as a rough individual: "I believe I am portrayed differently than I actually am; I believe I am portrayed in a rougher sense than the actual product. An actual product is a lot more mellow than the portrayal" (NBC News 2016). The commentator followed that statement: "And that may be his [Trump's] biggest asset of all. When people attack Trump, they reinforce the version of Trump that Trump wants people to see, and inevitably, that keeps Trump's name in the news" (NBC News 2016).

Trump, certainly, was not the first American president whose image was constructed around a tough guy core. The presidential job had long been seen as exemplary regarding this quality, and the degree of toughness has been commonly used as the measure of a politician's quality. It is a quality that is required across the political spectrum by Democrats and Republicans alike. Responding to a question on what makes a good president in a 1982 interview by Pat Buchanan, Richard Nixon went straight to the point: "I want one who, when the tough decisions are made is cold and tough and will make the right decision without the fear of failure" (CNN 2013). Bill Clinton on the Arsenio Hall Show in June 1992 (where he memorably played the saxophone, wearing dark sunglasses), received an ovation from the audience and a "wow" from Arsenio for a comment on the presidency he was seeking at the time: "It's a tough job, you've got to be a tough guy" (mytalkshowheroes 2017).

It became a common practice for the news to include the word "tough" and its derivatives in the title or a running line of an episode even with no relevance to the actual content; when the term is actually present in the content, it will sure be in the headlines and in the title, regardless of whether it represents the essence of the message the episode is intended to convey. Such, an article on US–China relations titled "Trump, Biden try to outdo each other on tough talk on China," opens, "China has fast become a top election issue as President Donald Trump and Democrat Joe Biden engage in a verbal brawl over who's better at playing the tough guy against Beijing" (Reichman and Lemire 2021), and then follows with an account of China–US relations as if the issue lay rather within the realm of the "tough talk" than actual politics. "The Trump administration was tougher than people give it credit for. And the Biden administration is also going to be pretty tough on the Russians," assessed Donald Jensen, a former US diplomat and a director for Russia and strategic stability at the US Institute of Peace (Wolfgang 2021). The title of an article about a situation with the resignation of John Bolton, nicknamed by Trump "Mr. Tough Guy," written by the US national security advisor and United States ambassador to the United Nations, again, includes the "tough" in it, and the major theme it set by Trump's caution: "In some cases he thought it was too tough what we were doing. Mr. Tough Guy, you know you have to go into Iraq" (McGraw 2019). A *New York Times* article, "The Toughest of the Tough Guys," about Marc Kasowitz, a personal outside lawyer for Donald Trump during his presidency, provides a concise account of Kasowitz's impressive professional encounters and yet follows the established media trend:

> The first paragraph of the online biography on his firm's website, before mentioning any of his work, cites the dozens of media outlets that have written about him, and how they have described him as the "toughest lawyer on Wall Street," an "uberlitigator" and "the toughest of the tough guys" (Sorkin 2017)

Even self-naming as a tough adds to a political image of a politician or a person who represents them (such as the lawyer), and the ability to "talk tough" is seen as a major political strength.

Admitting a politician's toughness usually indicates his or her acceptance to the political elite circle. Thus, *the Guardian* announced that Xi Jinping, President of the People's Republic of China, was admitted to the "tough guy" club (Tisdall 2017). President Biden, during the CNN presidential town hall in July of 2021, said of Xi Jinping, "He is a bright and really tough guy" (Clarke 2021). On the contrary, criticizing an opponent by proclaiming their lack of toughness can harm or even destroy their political ambitions. Also harmful is mocking a politician as "tough" while presenting them as, in fact, lacking that crucial quality, which occurred during an unforgettable exchange between Donald Trump and Jeb Bush during the CNN GOP debate, in 2015, when Trump's comment caused laughter in the audience.

Jeb Bush: "This is a tough business to run for president."
Trump, overspeaking: "Oh, yeah, you are a tough guy, Jeb."

"You are real tough, you are real tough," Trump repeated, continuing to talk over Bush saying: "You are never going to be a president of the United States by insulting your way to the presidency" (CNN 2015)—a meaningful and potentially memorable phrase that got lost in the excitement of the audience over the "tough" exchange. And the press reacted: "Donald Trump and Jeb Bush finally gave us the glorious manly-man brawl over 'toughness' we've all been waiting for" (Reeve 2015). This was one of many media reports picking on this short portion of a much longer conversation between the two. The notorious ending of Trump's letter to the president of Turkey, Recep Tayyip Erdogan, in October of 2019 ("Don't be a tough guy. Don't be a fool!" [Bowen 2019]) was meant to show that in the competition of toughness, Erdogan was losing to Trump, and it would be foolish to not recognize the defeat, not accept the deal Trump was offering.

Those are extremes in the demands of a politician to be tough, but between toughness and lack of toughness, a politician can slide along the scale, changing the degree of their toughness in response to the demands of the electorate and their sympathizers. Where toughness is seen as a virtue, the worthiness of a politician is assessed by where they fit on the scale of toughness. One of the ways to raise a politician's potency—and, of course, toughness—is assigning the tough qualities to an opponent or to the circumstances they have to deal with, especially when those are thought of to demonstrate toughness of a higher degree. Joe Biden clearly showed a recognition of this tactic when, during his meetings with NATO allies in Brussels in August of 2021, he called Putin "tough," "bright," and a "worthy adversary" (Rascoe 2021).

Vladimir Putin has firmly settled on "the toughest guy" end of the spectrum—"the hard man," "the tough-guy leader with a ruthless streak and a big ego," "a role model for the genre" (Tisdall 2017), who "doesn't mess around" (Hickey and Ingersoll 2013). Putin's image is being used as a solid, immutable reference point for all the motion along the axis of toughness and, forestalling, along the axis of goodness and badness. Dealing with Putin is commonly presented as the challenge, taking on which makes the most difficult trial for a politician and the most reliable proof of his or her fitness for the job. "I like Putin, he likes me," announced Trump; "the tougher and meaner" strongmen leaders are, "the better I get along with them" (Nigam 2021). Presenting Putin as tough is used to offer a challenge difficult enough to allow the biceps of the politician who is dealing with it to shine: taking on Putin serves as a proof of that politician's bravery and extraordinary toughness even if the attempted attack is merely verbal. Thus, Hillary Clinton went off the toughness chart when she called Putin a "tough guy with a thin skin" (Agence France Presse 2014).

Although Putin's toughness has become a touchstone in American and, to an extent, in a global political discourse, it is not a translation from how the Russian president is presented in the Russian media for the Russian people. His portrayals in the Western and the Russian media are in sharp contrast to each other. The pictures of Putin piloting a military aircraft, getting to the bottom of the ocean in a submarine, and, of course, riding a horse topless in the wildness of Siberia—those are only few examples of what could be and, probably, was thought to portray Putin as a tough character and what had become a part of the Western collective imagination. Among the Russian audience, however, those images did not quite bring the point across. At the very beginning of Putin's presidential career, there were significant attempts to develop the image of him as a tough character and a tough talker, but, as one of his imagemakers, Gleb Pavlovkiy, admitted, "He did not suit the role well" (Bekbulatova 2018). For example, Putin's statement in 1999 about those who bombed apartment houses in Moscow, "If we catch them in the toilet, we will rub them out in the outhouse" (Wines 2002), remains one of his most notorious and memorable phrases, but it was not impressive in the way it was thought to be when Putin was given the line. The phrase did not come across as tough but rather as near to inappropriate; it probably did not become comic only because of the tragic character of the event it related to, with its multiple casualties.

In the Russian media, Putin is presented as professional, patriotic, caring, adventurous (flying with the birds, diving in a submarine or scuba diving to "find" antique vases), emotional, "soft-spoken," chivalrous around women, adopting an especially friendly manner with children, and particularly respectful of the elderly: those and other qualities enforced by the media create a pool where the traits associated with toughness get lost. In fact, a lightly humorous and down-to-earth presentation of Putin as an ordinary citizen is a leading mode for the media to tell stories about him, regardless of the accuracy of such a presentation. One publication pictures Putin as a "sweet-tooth leader" who, during his annual visits to the MAKS aerospace show is, year after year, craving for an ice-cream bar but is only carrying bills on him too large for the saleswoman to give him a change, and thus he cannot get a longed-for ice-cream bar (Shakhova 2019). (He eventually figures that he can use a large bill to buy a whole lot of ice-cream bars and treat his entire entourage, so no change is needed.) In multiple articles and books, Andrey Kolesnikov, a journalist who receives special treatment in the Kremlin media pool, presents witty and absurdist-hilarious accounts of Putin's official performances. Video reports of Putin's job routine by Pavel Zarubin, a journalist, who has an unprecedented access to Putin and authors a weekly program, "Moscow. Kremlin. Putin," include unconventional, backstage shots of Putin, charged with a good dose of humor and the idea that Putin is no more than an ordinary man. Zarubin's program is co-hosted by Vladimir Soloviov, an odious journalist (many call him propagandist) on the pro-government channel "Russia-1," a clear sign that the way Putin is presented in Zarubin's program is officially approved and encouraged.

Thus, the contrast between the way the American and the Russian media present Putin is striking. If the American media aim to make the viewer overestimate the significance of Putin's persona and the power he possesses, the Russian media, on the contrary, tend to downplay his personal significance and present him as a less empowered figure than he probably is. Moreover, even language does not support the "tough" concept: there is no semantic equal to the term "tough" in Russian; various qualities that could constitute an equivalent to American "tough" do not merge in one word. Putin's toughness, undoubtedly, is a part not of Russian but of American political discourse, and its meaning and significance should be sought within the American political tradition.

Masculine politics and the origin of the tough

Any political message is sharpened to make a politician more successful than the competitors. In politics, a "traditionally masculine sphere" and "the most masculine of the human arts" (Hart 1994, 18), toughness became a marker of masculinity, and both being a man and being tough became traditional attributes of a national leader. This automatically declares at least half the population as not meant to succeed in politics because of their gender, reserving the political arena mainly for men—a theme thoroughly substantiated in feminist literature. The value assigned to "toughness" preserves the political sphere from intrusion by women and people of other genders and draws a demarcation line they are not supposed to cross; if they cross it, they might face greater challenges in fulfilling their political ambitions. With tough masculinity used as a marker of professional worthiness in the business of governing society, all who do not possess and overtly present this quality are in jeopardy of being screened out of the competition, regardless of their professional and personal virtues. A "less impressive man is a less impressive leader," so to be an effective politician, one is supposed to be "sufficiently masculine" (Harmer, Savigny, and Ward 2017, 968).

The "tough guy" claim not only screens out people of other genders but also leaves little room for other formats of masculinity, allowing only one version of manhood to dominate (Kimmel 2013). Michaele Kimmel (2013) noted that the dominance of one model was not inevitable, which is becoming more obvious with competition from other models of masculinity and other genders increasing. Even now, despite the growing diversity of and within genders, the projection of the image of traditional manhood remains "central to the job description of an American presidential candidate—especially in the Republican primaries" (Katz 2016, 242). When a presidential candidate does not connect with the electoral public based on his program or demographic characteristics such as race and class, gender becomes a point of sought connection. The stereotyped expression of manhood, inevitably oversimplified, is used as the last argument, and becomes a resort for relating to potential voters. That was the case with Richard Nixon, who, "egged on by his aides," "liked to play the tough guy" and declared that he hated spending time with intellectuals because "there's something feminine about them" (Thomas 2015). That was also the case with Ronald Reagan, who was "playing the role of the nation's leading man," with Mitt Romney—"man enough for the job" (Katz 2016, 224)—and, of course, with Donald Trump. Jackson Katz (2016) claimed that billionaires Mitt Romney and Donald Trump connected with their not-so-economically-powerful White base through their manhood; in Romney's case, though, this part was not nearly as enhanced as in Trump's. White, blue collar, heterosexual men, discounted of socioeconomic status and, as a result, of a certain degree of their masculinity, were thought to be the target audience susceptible to the excessively demonstrated toughness in presidential candidate. A collective overly simplified portrait of this group was successfully paired with the "cartoonish display of hyper-masculine posturing," "can-do confidence," "blunt talk," and "reality TV showmanship" (Katz 2016, 234) exhibited by presidential candidates.

In political debates, "emasculation of political rivals" and "attacking the masculinity of political opponents" are often used to devalue their leadership potency (Harmer, Savigny, and Ward 2017, 968). Dignam et al. (2021) argued that gendered self-presentation, exemplified in the "tough guy" image, helps presidential candidates secure political support grounded in the audience's interpretation. The study found that research participants perceived Trump's political incorrectness as masculine, as an evidence of his ability to exert and resist control, and as a peculiar way of outmasculinizing his opponents, both women and men (Digman et al. 2021).

Persistence, with which the vision of dominating masculinity is reproduced as the essence of political might, has an aspect that goes beyond the social dimension of power distribution. Rupert Wilkinson, the author of *American Tough* (1984), insisted that the tradition of presenting the "tough guy" masculinity as a criterion of political effectiveness lay within the domain of American national mythology. Wilkinson suggested that admiration of toughness rested, first, on a well-established "complex of frontier myth and imagery" and on the paradigm of American hero—the front man of the westward expansion. It was an encounter with the frontier where American character was crafted, where "posed against his environment was the guy who can took care of himself physically, economically, and socially" (Wilkinson 1984, 7). Challenges of the frontier life at the age of survival evoked in a man a multiplicity of traits, a particular combination of which constituted "body power and other kinds of toughness" (Wilkinson 1984, 11); those traits defined a heroic model for the nation in becoming. The tough masculinity, claimed Wilkinson, was physically defined; it was displayed in physical strength and in the size of the hero's body, matching the scale of the challenge the hero was overcoming. In support of this claim, Elliott West (1988) observed that actors starring in leading roles in the Westerns in the 1930 through the 1950s were all "oversized" men, the size of their body signaling their outstanding ability to intimidate a resistant environment and stand against other various challenges.

Wilkinson pinpointed two other interrelated sources of American preoccupation with toughness that contributed to the rise of the tough-man cult. The first of those two sources were the opposition of the West and the East as two ways of life and social organization, with the West seen as pure, simple, and heroic and the East seen as outlived, corrupted, and unnecessarily complicated. The second source was the voluntary austerity of the Western man in opposition to influences of a prosperous and excessive East, which was equalized with the social and spiritual ills of the metropolis: "In the patriotic and puritan view, proper American traits were essentially un-European or un-British" (Wilkinson 1984, 99). The frontierer was "a plain man, anti-courtier tradition that goes back to Tudor and Stuart England"—a "negative reference point for American identity" (Wilkinson 1984, 9). According to this view, the "plain man" resolved the "tension between striving and self-indulgence" in favor of intentional ascetism; he did so, in part, in response to severe conditions, but mainly because the austerity was his zone of comfort and a core characteristic that enabled him to sustain the challenge of the absence of civilization at the first place.

> Befitting the new nation forged in moral hope amid the wilderness, the true American was vigorous, manly, and direct, not effete and corrupt like the supposed Europeans. He was plain rather than ornamented, rugged rather than luxury-seeking, a liberty-loving common man or natural gentleman rather than an aristocratic oppressor or servile minion.
> (Wilkinson 1984, 95–96)

If the tough guy concept became a core of the Western frontier myth, the myth itself became the core of American nation-building mythology. Basic American values and ideologies, directly related to the frontier experiences and memories, produced the multiplicity of meanings and strategies of building national identity around this core. "No other nation has taken a time and place from its past and produced a construct of imagination equal to America's creation of the West," commented David Murdoch (2001, vii) on the significance of the frontier myth in the construction of American nation. The frontier myth "established itself in American culture as the most persuasive structure for interpreting America's past" and "became guideposts for the present and a vision to inspire the future," elaborated David Smith (2021, 56–57) on this idea.

Although the story of the frontier has served as a major culture metaphor and a means of harmonizing social behavior, Americans' response to the tough-guys models was not homogeneous:

> Some honor them wholeheartedly and on the most part consistently. Others do so more sporadically, often with conjunctions with styles that are not at all tough. Still others develop wholly different modes of behavior, sometimes in reaction *against* the tough guy. Even so, notions of dynamic toughness represent a cultural force with which virtually all Americans have to deal in some way.
>
> (Wilkinson 1984, 5)

Wilkinson affirmed that the "mixture of silence and ambiguity has nowhere appeared more vividly than in journalistic debates about the merits of presidents and presidential candidates" (Wilkinson 1984, 5). The frontier mythology as a uniting narrative for the nation has been deeply embedded in American presidential politics, which boldly exploited the theme of toughness, masculinity, and the frontier in constructing images of presidents as all-national heroes (see Smith 2021). Presidents have been elevated to "demigods" (Erikson 1985, 3) with archetypal characteristics assigned to them (Hankins 1983, 267). "Counting approximately from Teddy Roosevelt right to the present day, Americans have liked to link their presidents with the West, with Westerns, with big cowboy hats," combining in the presidential image "the leader of the Western world and the Wild West" folklore (Wertheimer 2008). When Byron Price, head curator of the "Cowboys and Presidents" exhibition at the Autry National Center in 2008 was asked, "What is it about America's politics that cries out for a cowboy identity for our presidents?" and why do "Americans link their commanders in chief to the cowboys of the Wild West?" he responded, "Cowboys represent masculinity, bravery, courageousness, selflessness, rugged individualism. . . . Its appeal is especially strong during periods of national crisis and trauma, whether it'd be war or depression, because cowboys appeal to strength, stability and core values" (ibid.).

David Smith (2021), the author of a recently published *Cowboy-Presidents: The Frontier Myth and U.S. Politics Since 1900*, introduced a line of presidents whose imagery demonstrated references to cowboyhood and "personal ties to the frontier myth" (Smith 2021, 15): Theodore Roosevelt, Lyndon Johnson, Ronald Reagan, and George W. Bush. Each of the listed "cowboy presidents" exploited specific aspects of the cowboy image, a major point of interest to Smith. Not all of them, however, represented distinctive characteristics of the hero that mark and personify the milestones, the turning points in the frontier mythology. The following chapters intend to track the logic of the progression of the frontier myth through presidential politics and three milestones of this development: at the moment of the myth's becoming with Theodore Roosevelt; at the height of its development with Ronald Reagan; and in its latest transformation and upgrade with the entrance to the big politics of Donald Trump.

References

Agence France Presse. 2014. "Hillary Clinton Says Putin 'Can Be Dangerous' and 'Always Goes to the Limits'." *Insider*, July 7. www.businessinsider.com/hillary-clinton-talks-about-putin-2014-7.
AmericanShows. 2013. "Donald Trump on David Letterman. Full Interview." October 22. www.youtube.com/watch?v=PR_SoJpWzOA.
Bekbulatova, Taisia. 2018. "Dissident, Kotory Stal Ideologom Putina: Polnaya Istoria Gleba Pavlovskogo—Cheloveka, Pridumavshego Sovremennuyu Rossiyskuyu Vlast." *Meduza*, July 9. https://meduza.io/feature/2018/07/09/dissident-kotoryy-stal-ideologom-putina.
Bowen, Jeremy. 2019. "Turkey's Erdogan 'Threw Trump's Syria Letter in Bin'." *BBC*, October 17. www.bbc.com/news/world-middle-east-50080737.
Clarke, Tyrone. 2021. "Biden Labels Xi Jinping 'Bright' and a 'Really Tough Guy'." *Sky News Australia*, July 22. www.skynews.com.au/world-news/united-states/president-joe-biden-says-chinese-dictator-xi-jinping-is-a-bright-and-really-tough-guy/news-story/beaa346323f7504bc295098ddd9ab3d0.
CNN. 2013. "Nixon with No Expletives Deleted." *CNN*, July 31. www.youtube.com/watch?v=MacmN1EtIPQ.
———. 2015. "Donald Trump: 'Oh, You're a Tough Guy, Jeb'." Filmed during the CNN GOP debate, 0:26, December 15. www.youtube.com/watch?v=3MdIri5ji68.
Dignam, Pierce, Douglas Schrock, Kristen Erichsen, and Benjamin Dowd-Arrow. 2021. "Valorizing Trump's Masculine Self: Constructing Political Allegiance during the 2016 Presidential Election." *Men and Masculinities* 21 (3). doi:10.1177/1097184X19873692.
Erikson, Paul. 1985. *Reagan Speaks*. New York: New York University Press.
Hankins, Sarah. 1983. "Archetypal Alloy: Reagan's Rhetorical Image." *Central States Speech Journal* 34 (1): 33–43. doi:10.1080/10510978309368112.
Harmer, Emily, Heather Savigny, and Orlanda Ward. 2017. "'Are You Tough Enough?' Performing Gender in the UK Leadership Debates 2015." *Media, Culture & Society* 39 (7): 960–75. doi:10.1177/0163443716682074.
Hart, Roderick P. 1994. *Seducing America: How Television Charms the Modern Voter*. New York: Oxford University Press.
Hickey, Walter, and Geoffrey Ingersoll. 2013. "43 Photos Showing Vladimir Putin Doesn't Mess Around." *Business Insider*, September 6. www.businessinsider.in/43-photos-showing-vladimir-putin-doesnt-mess-around/articleshow/22375488.cms.
Katz, Jackson. 2016. *Man Enough? Donald Trump, Hilary Clinton, and the Politics of Presidential Masculinity*. Northampton, Massachusetts: Interlink Publishing Group, Inc.
Kimmel, Michael. 2013. *Angry White Men: American Masculinity at the End of an Era*. New York: Nation Books.

McGraw, Meridith. "Trump Says He Split with 'Mr. Tough Guy' Bolton Over 'Very Big Mistakes'." *ABC News*, September 11. https://abcnews.go.com/Politics/trump-split-mr-tough-guy-bolton-big-mistakes/story?id=65544651.

Murdoch, David H. 2001. *The American West: The Invention of Myth*. Cardiff: Welsh Academic Press.

mytalkshowheroes. 2017. "Bill Clinton on 'ARSENIO'—1992." *MyTalkShowHeroes*, video 8:08. www.youtube.com/watch?v=y1xFovBCe6A.

NBC News. 2016. "1980s: How Donald Trump Created Donald Trump." *NBC News*, Filmed video 4:51, July. www.youtube.com/watch?v=_FLo14GMYos.

Nigam, Aanchal. 2021. "'Cold Dude': Ahead of Biden–Putin Meet, a Look at Remarks of Former POTUS on Russian Prez." *Republic World*, June 15. www.republicworld.com/world-news/us-news/cold-dude-ahead-of-biden-putin-meet-a-look-at-remarks-of-former-potus-on-russian-prez.html.

Rascoe, Ayesha. 2021. "Biden Says Russia's Putin Is a 'Worthy Adversary' Whether or Not He Trusts Him." *NPR*, June 14. www.npr.org/2021/06/14/1006282205/biden-says-russias-putin-is-a-worthy-adversary-whether-or-not-he-trusts-him.

Reeve, Elspeth. 2015. "Donald Trump and Jeb Bush Finally Gave Us the Glorious Manly-Man Brawl Over 'Toughness' We've All Been Waiting for." *CNN*, December 15.

Reichman, Deb, and Jonathan Lemire. 2021. "Trump, Biden Try to Outdo Each Other on Tough Talk on China." *AP News*, July. https://apnews.com/article/025d0fea834a4c0c60b33fe56e632758.

Shakhova, Anna. 2019. "Sladkaya Zhyzn: Na Chto Putin Tratit Svoyu Zarplatu. Dnevnik Raskhodov Prezidenta." *Secret Firmy*, September 6. https://secretmag.ru/news/chto-putin-kupil-na-svoyu-zarplatu.htm.

Smith, David. 2021. *Cowboy Presidents: The Frontier Politics and US Myth Since 1990*. Norman, OK: University of Oklahoma Press.

Sorkin, A. 2017. "Trump's Lawyer, Marc Kasowitz: 'The Toughest of the Tough Guys'." *The New York Times*, June 5. www.nytimes.com/2017/06/05/business/dealbook/sorkin-marc-kasowitz-trump-lawyer.html.

Thomas, Evan. 2015. "The Complexity of Being Richard Nixon." *The Atlantic*, June 15. www.theatlantic.com/politics/archive/2015/06/the-complexity-of-being-richard-nixon/394547/.

Tisdall, Simon. 2017. "Trump, Putin and Xi: A Year of Tough-Guy Leaders and Foolish Brinkmanship." *The Guardian*, December 25. www.theguardian.com/world/2017/dec/25/trump-putin-and-xi-a-year-of-tough-guy-leaders-and-foolish-brinkmanship.

Wertheimer, Linda. 2008. "Exhibit Explores Cowboy–President Connection." *NPR*. July 12, 2008. https://www.npr.org/templates/story/story.php?storyId=92489084

West, Elliott. 1988. "Shots in the Dark: Television and the Western Myth." *Montana: The Magazine of Western History* 38 (2): 72–76. www.jstor.org/stable/4519136.

Wilkinson, Rupert. 1984. *American Tough: The Tough Guy Tradition and American Character*. New York: Perennial Library.

Wines, Michael. 2002. "Did Putin Really Say That? Oh Yes." *New York Times News Service*. *Chicago Tribune*. November 13, 2002. https://www.chicagotribune.com/news/ct-xpm-2002-11-13-0211103081-story.html

Wolfgang, Ben. 2021. "Sharply Critical, Biden Now Tracks Trump on Russia Policy." *The Washington Times*, May 26. www.washingtontimes.com/news/2021/may/26/sharply-critical-biden-now-tracks-trump-russia-pol/.

2 Theodore Roosevelt
The becoming of the frontier and the arrival of the hero

Performative frontier: staging the myth

The Western frontier was fated to become a theme in presidential politics. When, in the 1840 presidential election, the Whig party candidate William Harry Harrison—the first American president who campaigned actively for office—was mocked by his Democratic opponents as too old for the presidency and only capable of enjoying retirement in a log cabin with a barrel of a hard cider, the Whig party turned the table around and declared Harrison "the log cabin and hard cider candidate" (Library of Congress n.d.). That move converted a losing trait into a virtue and presented Harrison, a descendant of rich Virginian aristocratic families (unlike his opponent Van Buren, who was indeed coming from a poor, working family) as "a simple frontier Indian fighter," "a man of the common people from the rough-and-tumble West" (The White House n.d.). It was the first actively run American presidential campaign (Library of Congress n.d.) with a slogan, a campaign song, and other symbolic attributes that turned out to be operational in diverting public attention away from discussing real issues, such as those of slavery and of the national bank.

Theodore Roosevelt took the office 60 years later, and he, too, was a financially secure Easterner running his presidential campaign on the frontier theme. Unlike Harrison, who was forced toward the log cabin image to compensate for the creativity of his opponents, Roosevelt, "that cowboy in the office," took the initiative in exploiting the frontier theme consciously and early in his political career.

By the time Roosevelt articulated his political ambitions, the transformation of the reality of the frontier into a story, and then into a myth, had already been happening for decades. With the Western territories and the resistance of their native inhabitants gradually retreating before the colonization efforts, the frontier was fading as an actual landscape and reappearing as a set of stories and imageries. Those stories and imageries were informed by real events, circumstances, and personalities, yet the meanings borrowed from the reality were rearranged and the reality was deconstructed and corrected, infused with

DOI: 10.4324/9781003415312-2

the great amount of "overactive and sensational imagination" (Goetzmann and Goetsmann 2009, 288).

Himself a "mythic Westerner" (Hankins 1983, 274), "a cowboy out west and governor in the east" (Smith 2021, 52), Theodore Roosevelt combined the authenticity of the wilderness and the heroism of the frontier with the institutional autocriticism of supreme executive power. He was one of the last who could capitalize on a personal exposure to the frontier life; he was also the first to exploit the frontier myth in its clear articulation and to make it an unbeaten theme in politics. Moreover, Roosevelt happened to be at the epicenter of the creative efforts directed to constructing the mythology of American West, and, because of his empowered position, he found himself, to an extent, coordinating those cross-fertilizing (White 1994) efforts. He was himself one of the most active creators of the myth, by living the West, by his Western-inspired military and law-enforcement activities, by his writings, and by his appeal to the most prominent members of the creative cohort, who worked to reestablish the rough reality of the frontier into an abstracted, aestheticized, and romanticized mythic West. As David Murdoch put it: "Roosevelt made the West which made him" (Murdoch 2001, 71).

In the West painted by Albert Bierstadt, Frederic Remington, John Muir, and Charles Russel, the rocks of Yosemite were even mightier, the open plains of Wyoming were even wider, and the cowboy life was detailed, vibrant, relatable, evoking vivid empathy, including in those who had never been even remotely exposed to the reality of handling cattle. As the real West was being gradually peopled "by the immigrants from the old European World . . . the West of the imagination" (Goetzmann and Goetzmann 1986)—a beautified revision of itself—was being built by a collective effort of artists, writers, and performers as a special, secure, and indoctrinating cradle for American national conciseness.

The dime novel, a common read though most of the 19th century, also presented a romanticized version of the West and of the Westerner. The dime novel cowboy could, at least on the pages of an affordable copy, depart from the routine, loneliness, and hardship of his day-to-day duties into the dream world of a man of an archetypal scale and action. Smith (2021) noted that "the dime-novel cowboy" "apparently had nothing to do with cattle" and was preoccupied, instead, with catching the outlaws and helping the weaker (Smith 2021, 113). As the dime novel was building the readership across the nation, the imaginary cowboy was drifting from his real-life job description to assuming a heroic character, from watching and directing the flock to fixing justice and setting the social order.

Those short novels were borrowing from folkways and adventures of the frontier men and returning their extreme experiences, refurnished and turned into even more extreme as simplified, standardized formulaic action stories with modeled personalities and behaviors. In the novels, the world of hardworking men was brighter, their clothes were cleaner, the choices were easier to make, women were more available and agreeable, the outlaws were easier to defeat, and fame and recognition were faster to obtain. It was the dream world of an escape, where a man could skip the everyday routine of hard work and jump right into a one-time heroic action that would bring him the recognition of his outstanding personal features. When Theodore Roosevelt—the "four-eyed Eastern dude"—appeared in the Dakota Territory in a specially tailored Western outfit, too fancy for his local companions to ever afford, with a handcrafted rifle and a hunting knife from Tiffany & Co. of New York, the locals accepted this version of the Westerner as an upgraded but legitimate enough representation of their own generalized character.

Other literary forms were contributing as well, allowing for more sophistication to the character and the plot compared with the short format of the dime novel. Owen Wister, Roosevelt's Harvard clubmate and friend, wrote *The Virginian* (1902), the pioneering Western novel, not without encouragement from Roosevelt, who Wister called his "dear critic" and to whom he dedicated the book. Whether Wister looked for any insights in Roosevelt's Western experience or had had enough of his own from spending several summers in the Territory of Wyoming, the drama set by Wister in *The Virginian* clicked with Roosevelt's personal attachments and presented the aesthetics, for which public admiration was growing. *The Virginian* set major elements of the Western genre and contributed to already established practice of turning novels into staged performances. Two years after its first publication, it was adapted for the stage and, in another decade, for the screen.

The Virginian was neither the only nor the first literary product turned into a stage performance. Besides a vivid exchange between literary forms and the stage, the characters were traveling easily between the pages, the stages, and their real-life ventures. A published account of Buffalo Bill's adventures in the West, for which the author Ned Buntline used the name and some character traits of Buffalo Bill Cody but added lots of made-up details, landed on the stage of a popular Chicago playhouse in 1872 (Goetzmann and Goetzmann 1986, 289); the outstanding part in the "poorly acted," "written in four hours" melodrama *The Scouts of the Prairie* (ibid., 287) was that of Bill Cody himself, who, accompanied by another recognizable personality, Texas Jack Omohundro, arrived from the audience on stage at the most dramatic moment to lasso and defeat the villains. Plays known as "border dramas" that Buffalo Bill Cody was staging for a decade after his debut in *The Scouts of the Prairie*, "featuring genuine frontier characters, real Indians, fancy shooting, and sometimes horses" (Fees n.d.), finally took off as the Wild West Show, the outdoor reconstruction of the western life, to which "Cody gave a dramatic narrative structure" (Fees n.d.). Buffalo Bill Cody compacted the dramatic history of the West into several hours of a plotted action staged on several acres of land, with a group of presenters impersonating various character types from both sides of the frontier. Richard White (1994, 1) affirmed this: "although fictional, Buffalo Bill's story claimed to represent a history"; it "defined the popular image of the West for many Americans" who were convinced they were witnessing "an authentic depiction of the Wild West" (White 1994). The "genuine characters" presenting themselves, such as "hunters, cowboys, marksmen, and even the Native Americans" (ibid.) were supplying the staged act with authenticity.

Theodore Roosevelt had a finger in the pie when he made legendary Geronimo and five other Indian warriors participate in the 1905 inauguration parade to, as he put it, "give people a real show" (Binkovitz 2013). Roosevelt did not shy away from dramatizations, as with the well-known 1886 picture of him guarding the boat thieves he had just chased down and captured, a story he described in *Ranch Life and the Hunting Trail*; Roosevelt did not have his camera with him to document the event, so he staged the scene later with his companions performing as the captured thieves. Neither did Roosevelt hold back from facilitating an exchange between the fantasy and the reality, as when he borrowed the term "Rough Riders" from Buffalo Bill's Wild West Show to name the 1st United States Volunteer Cavalry, a regiment he raised in 1898 to fight in the Spanish-American War. It was a multistep transaction, a myth–reality acrobatic sketch: in 1893, Buffalo Bill enacted in the Congress of Rough Riders of the World show his long-term fantasy about rough, militarized masculinity of the men riding and guarding the borders of the old American West; then Roosevelt borrowed the name for the real military unit and adopted it as a title for his 1899 military memoirs; and then, in 1900, Buffalo Bill reappropriated the term and the image, by that time already infused with a real experience of a military regiment, to reenact in his show one of the most dramatic events of the war that regiment participated in, the taking of San Juan Hill. Buffalo Bill even recruited 16 of Roosevelt's Rough Riders to participate in the reenactment, bringing, again, real characters to perform as themselves in a show.

And, of course, there was an academic input into the collective mythmaking effort by a historian, Frederick Turner, a paper *The Significance of the Frontier in American History*, presented at the 1893 American Historical Association (AHA) meeting. The announcement of the 1890 Census closure of the Western frontier caused Turner to reflect on its role in the formation of American institutions and national character, and the *Frontier Thesis* has since been regarded as the classic articulation of frontier mythology.

The eighth meeting of the American Historical Association, which should have been held in December of 1892, was postponed to the summer of the next year to coincide with the opening of the World's Columbian Exposition (the Chicago World Fair), a grandiose celebration of the 400th anniversary of Columbus' arrival in America. It is likely that Turner's choice of the subject for his thesis was predefined by the 400-year milestone in American history and the AHA's attention to it. The meeting itself was a part of the World Congress Auxiliary of the World's Columbia Exposition that "intended to provide a scholarly contrast to the popular pleasures of the fair's 'Midway Plaisance'"

(Hauss 2004). With this objective in mind, the AHA worked its schedule around the Fair: all morning sessions were to be "brief [so] members can have abundant time each day for visiting the Columbian Exposition" (ibid.). The agenda was related to the event, too.

Featuring a newly invented, electricity-powered Ferris wheel and electrically lighted buildings—"temples to industry and civilization, templates for banks and public buildings across the country" (The Editors of Encyclopedia Britannica 2023), attended by approximately 27 million people—an equivalent of one in four Americans (Roosevelt 1899), the Fair was a prospect into a glorious future and enough of an event to be represented on the Chicago flag as one of, then, two stars. Delivered on the premises of the White City, specially erected for the exhibition, Turner's thesis was probably not so much about the lost frontier as about the completion of a great historical period and the opening toward a new, even greater, future. Turner was announcing not the end of the story, but its major milestone, the turning point.

Although the World's Fair grounds, "spread over 686 acres along the city's south lakefront area," offered the awe of the materialized City Beautiful, adjoining it, between 62nd and 63rd Streets, was the booming Wild West Show of Buffalo Bill. With "two performances daily, 3 and 8 pm, rain or shine," the show was competing with the Fair for visitors, revenue, and the meanings of the frontier. As Richard White (1994) put it:

> Turner and Buffalo Bill told separate stories; indeed, each contradicted the other in significant ways. Turner's history was one of free land, the essentially peaceful occupation of a largely empty continent, and the creation of a unique American identity. Cody's Wild West told of violent conquest, of wresting the continent from the American Indian peoples who occupied the land. Although fictional, Buffalo Bill's story claimed to represent a history, for, like Turner, Buffalo Bill worked with real historical events and real historical figures.
>
> (White 1994)

Roosevelt, at that time a US Civil Service Commissioner, not only visited the exhibition but sponsored, through his Boone and Crockett Foundation, one of the attractions. The Hunter's Cabin, a replica of a typical pioneer house from the mid-19th century that contained a display of relics of Davy Crockett, appealed to the bygone past rather than the future. Crockett, bynamed "The King of the Wild Frontier," was a prototype of the hero of an immensely popular play by Kirke Paulding, *The Lion of the West*, as well as of a popular comic *Davy Crockett's Almanac*; Crockett's life—both real and imaginary—was written into multiple biographic accounts presenting "the adventures of the legendary Davy rather than the historical David Crockett" (Lofaro n.d.). Davy Crockett was an ambitious frontiersman with serious political aspirations mythologized into a folk hero—a figure to whom Roosevelt could definitely relate and references to whom he could incorporate into his own image. Whether the exhibit was planned to draw an association between Roosevelt and Crockett, or whether Roosevelt initiated it merely for the love of history, the frontier cabin containing personal items of a legendary frontier figure was likely to support the connections Roosevelt was working to establish between himself and the heroic myth of the Wild West.

In the dramatized, exaggerated, meaning-altered imaginary West, "the show and lived historical reality constantly imitated each other" (White 1994). Michael Rogin (1987) called this phenomenon of merging the reality and the story into an undividable holism of myth "boundary confusion." Rogin used the term to characterize the rhetorical power of Ronald Reagan, who, decades after Roosevelt, took the myth to a whole different level, relying upon his own screen-produced image and communicative talent. Roosevelt, however, was the one who established the practice of the mutual trespassing of the reality and the story and made it into a means of killing several birds with one stone: creating national myth, presenting the president's story as a perfect personification of the mythic character, and using those two for political marketing and promoting his own presidential image.

The enduring contradiction of myth

Despite the established "boundary confusion" between the reality of the frontier and the story of it, there were major discrepancies between the two.

First, the American "Wild" West was never a true wildness. Much of the territory in question was an inhabited, cared for, hunted on, cultivated, and symbolically acculturated, sanctified land. "Virgin land" was a helpful metaphor in providing an excuse for the conquest to be thought of as an exploration and for the resistance of the native population to be thought of as a mere obstacle in westward advancement. Given this shift in the meaning the metaphor allowed, the frontier was a divisive line between the meanings the Europeans enclosed in the western advancement and the meanings of this process on the other side of the divisible line—the experiences of the native inhabitants of the land. It was a line that, when crossed, turned comprehension of the experience into its justification, into an ideology.

Second, there was a discrepancy in the pace of progression in populating different areas of the land, as well as in the symbolic value assigned to populating of those different areas. Will Wright (1975) pointed to the disproportionally high attention given to the Western frontier compared with other parts of the country and, furthermore, within the American West, a disproportional emphasis on some periods of the westward progression compared with others:

> The great Texas cattle drives to the Kansas cow towns, the inspiration for much of the Western myth, lasted only from 1866 to 1885. . . . The crucial period of settlement in which most Westerns take placated only

about 30 years, from 1860 to 1990. . . . Even if we include the period of the California gold rush and the first wagon trains to Oregon, the entire period of western settlement lasted less than 50 years. . . . In contrast, the settling of the Eastern frontier—from the Atlantic to the Great Plains—required at least 130 years.

But "this era is not rich in mythical figures and events," and its heroes

> have a minor status in the modern imagination compared with the cowboys, gunfighters, and gamblers of the golden West. . . . In spite of its actual more prolonged adventure, the East could never match the social turmoil of the West as a context for fiction and . . . a ground for myth.
> (Wright 1975, 5–6)

Wright explained the reason for such an incongruity by two major factors. The first was temporal and cultural compression, an unprecedented variety of occupations and culture types present in the West

> in a remarkably compressed period. . . . For a brief time, many ways of life were available, each of which contend its own element of adventure. . . . And the variety of livelihoods allows for clear-cut conflicts of interests and values.
> (Wright 1975 5, 6)

Another factor, Wright claimed, was the usage of violence in settling those occupational and cultural differences.

Third, the frontier was a place "that is not, really, on any map" (West 1988, 39). Not a place on its own but a divide between the two areas of control—the wilderness and the land maintained by the civilizing hand of a farmer, it was a line where the qualities of the two sides met but did not mix, a point of transformation, a misplaced setting. It was not so much a landscape but a series of opportunities to realize and threats to face down (West 1988, 44), more of a story to tell than of an actual place to be, "the border between a world of possibilities and one of actualities, a world theoretically unlimited and one defined by its limitations" (Slotkin 1985, 45). Used to define a territory with a shifting location, or with no certain location, the term "frontier" itself was, as Frederick Turner (1966) mentioned, not well defined. Turner called it an "elastic" term with no "sharp definition" to describe the "outer edge," "the meeting point between savagery and civilization." Although deprived of a definite location, this imaginary place of escape created "an instantly recognizable context" (West 1988, 39) and established a major frame for the new, rising identity, and for a new format of the worldview.

Finally, there was no one frontier but a succession of drastically changing conditions and experiences of the generations of the colonists on their way westward. The progression of the frontier, or, rather, of the rolling forward and redefined frontiers, was accompanied with the increasing diversity of occupations and lifestyles on the settled territories. If crossing the frontier was the "initiation into new world and a new life that is at the core of the American experience" (Slotkin 1973, 52), crossing the progressing frontier was a progressing experience, all-embracing and diverse enough to produce a full-bodied, all-national story accumulated under a single name.

While the frontier was rolling forward and the experiences were multiplying, the story was developing in the opposite direction, toward an abstract and unifying narrative refined of specificities. The diversifying frontier was turning into an increasingly generalized image of itself. The complexity of the experiences was, nevertheless, preserved within that highly abstracted structure—not in its entire volume and complexity, but as a mere outline, as two poles, as the opposites, such as wilderness and civilization, East and West, good and bad, and, with regard to people, as settlers and worriers, hard workers and adventurers, outlaws and the men of virtue.

The discrepancies did not destroy the story's impact. On the contrary, they took the story to a new level, where it acquired the features of myth. Tolerance to opposites is specific to myth, as well as inpersonification of those opposites and acting them out. The steadiness of myth and the rigidity of its structure are predefined by the resistance of the opposites to resolute, by their fixation in mutually excluding qualities. As Wendy Doniger phrased it in a foreword to Levi-Strauss' *Myth and Meaning*: "Every myth is driven by the obsessive need to solve a paradox that cannot be solved" (Doniger 1995, x); or, as Janice Rushing cited Jenni Calder: "myth absorbs the inevitable contradictions without reconciling them . . . , strengthens the . . . archetype by revitalizing both aspects of the paradox as well as the . . . tension between them" (Rushing 1983, 21). Myth presents externalized oppositions fixed at their maximum, stretched to their limits, tension "to the breaking point." The characters impersonate the opposites and enact their relations, never reconciling; thus the opposites only make sense in their relations, as a contradiction within one essence, within one story.

"Myth is not whole when the audience is induced to identify with only one of its opposing values" (Rushing 2009, 22). The holistic essence of myth is maintained via the ongoing relations between the characters and via appropriation by the audience of the story the characters play. The struggle of the oppositions, interrelated and intertwined through their dramatic relations, produces both the structure and the inner developmental impulse; the impulse unfolds into existence within the forming structure. Within that structure and through the showdown between the agencies and characters as impersonalized oppositions arises the inner contradiction that resolves itself in a new essence. Thus, myth is the means of creating a new essence, it is a necessary stage in the becoming of a new reality, and that is fully applied to national identity and nation as such. The formation of a new nation implies the necessity of myth as the mechanism of its becoming.

The reality of the frontier's life, its uncertainty and novelty, called for a structure within which it could be ordered and comprehended. The social order with its regulating mechanisms was still to be established, and myth became an agency that suggested, provided the structure to the content that, due to its novelty, did not yet have its own. Thanks to its rigidity, myth supplied the framing that helped deal with overwhelming complexity, with potential or actual conflicts within the socially diverse, tense environment with a high level of uncertainty both within society and on the line between society and nature. Mythologization of the West reduced a turbulent complexity of the sociocultural experiences to basic mental oppositions, establishing for the people of various cultural and professional backgrounds clear markers of acceptable behaviors and morals.

The ordering and clarifying power of myth comes from its capacity to present the inner complexity as externalized oppositions and, further, present those externalized oppositions as independent entities with their own agencies as acting characters. The contradictions that constitute the myth structure are impersonated, and the story lays itself out as a plot with the hero getting into relations with other characters, whether those represent people, animals, gods, or the features of the environment. The characters form relations, and those relations, not the opposites impersonated by them, become the major point of the story. The shift of the focus from the opposites to their correlation turns the hero into a function of the story, and the story moves toward becoming the story of something else, of what the hero, through his struggle against other forces, brought to existence. Not the hero himself becomes important, but the traits he demonstrates by his action and incorporates into his physical and mental being. In the severe conditions of the frontier, the most valuable qualities were those that ensured physical survival, those we think of as features of the tough guy, so being tough was (in disagreement with the grammar) not as much a quality as it was a function that was transforming the oppositions of myth into a new essence, into a new identity.

Elliott West (1988) appealed to this quality of myth to present and preserve an ultimate contradiction and carry it through the story unresolved, when he wrote about the "schizophrenic element" of the frontier myth. In *Childhood and Society*, Erik Erikson regarded the manifestation of that same quality in what he called the American character or American identity: "whatever one may come to consider a truly American trait can be shown to have its equally characteristic opposite . . . with more extreme contrasts" (Erikson 1993, 244). Erikson specified that the said would be true of all national characters and added, "a nation's identity is derived from the ways in which history has, as it were, counterpointed certain opposite potentialities" (ibid. 285). In one of his *Letters from the West*, written back in the 1820s and titled *The National Character*, James Hall asserted, "The foreigners err when they give a character to our whole population from observations made in a single sea-pot, . . . because they discover traits in different places which seem to be very antipodes of each other" (Hall 1828, 238). Will Wright (1975) wrote about myth as the double essence of real experiences and a cognitive structure: "an abstract structure through which the human mind imposes a necessary order, and a symbolic content through which the formal structure is applied to contingent, socially defined experience" (Wright 1975, 11). From Wright's perspective, myth could be seen as the initial mode of cognitive development and, in the case of national identity (national character), a stage where the reflective ability is formed.

Now, having looked at the formative value of the frontier myth, let us take a look at its content.

The land and the man

In the frontier story, land was inseparably coupled with the man, whose mission was to transform it from wild to lived. The land provided the challenge, and the man—the hero of the story—provided an agency able to deal with that challenge. As James W. Steele wrote in *The Sons of the Border: Sketches of the Life and People on the Far Frontier*: "The Borderer is a man not born, but unconsciously to himself, *made* by his surroundings and necessities" (Steele 1873, 2).

The qualities of the land defined the qualities of the man, and the progression of the frontiers echoed in the progression of the man. He had to fight his way forward through the harsh conditions, and the harsher those conditions were, the more outstanding were the qualities of the man. The Rocky Mountains in the paintings of American landscapes were oversized, and their impressive qualities were otherwise exaggerated, for their might was raising the stakes for the man, who was surmounting them, thus raising the merits of the man. Through the clash between human might and the severe, inhumane conditions of the wilderness arose an exceptional set of features suitable for modeling the national character. The story of the frontier (the way it was told) was the story of power gradually taken by man from the wilderness in a struggle serious enough to toughen him to mythic proportions and craft him into a hero: "Superhumans, self-glorifying Americans, pioneers" were transforming "the pristine wilderness" of the plains into the Jeffersonian Garden (Bowden 1992, 3), the land of crops, domesticated animals, and homemade foods. The vision of this transformation was a guiding and mobilizing force; it also became a major narrative to utilize in the domain of governing.

The contrast of the two landscapes was replicated as the contrast of human types inhabiting the two sides of the divide: an actual frontier man, who was dealing with the wilderness, and those who followed him to the conquest territories and who actually planted the dreamed-of Jeffersonian garden—a settler, a farmer, a townsman—the whole spectrum of the occupations and social connections that grew in number and complexity with the progression of the frontier. Mirroring the relativism of the frontier line was the intersection between the frontier man and the settler: the earlier could settle down on the inhabitable side of the divide, and the later could leave his peaceful occupation to protect his already cultivated land and established relations with his family and the community. Although actual people could switch between these two roles, the roles themselves were strictly defined and fixed constants in the story. The demarcation line between the two characters was so rigid and switching from one role to another was so dramatic that, until now, the drama of a person facing the necessity of moving from one role to the other constitutes one of the most popular plots in the Western genre.

In the meanwhile, myth was further presenting a deepening contradiction of the abstract and concrete. The growing diversity of the occupations, lifestyles, and characters driven by diversifying conditions and by the "local circumstances—climate, soil, and institutions" (Hall 1828, 234) made it increasingly difficult for one of the many occupations and associated cultural models to become or remain representative of all. The unifying image of the frontiersman was torn apart by the many types of actual people whom this term was meant to describe. At the same time, the frontier hero would not be able to deal with all the variety of challenges, should his skills be narrowed down to a particular occupation. Just as the experiences of the frontier were abstracted from its historically defined qualities into a single word, the leading character, the hero of the myth had to also be abstracted from the multiplicity of the occupations and lifestyles with only essential, basic traits remaining. In response to this contradictory demand, the hero's characteristics were becoming, simultaneously, more abstract and more concrete. As the frontier was becoming a story more than a real land, as it was absorbing under one word continuingly multiplying experiences, the real hero was (becoming) "an idea rather than a person" (Griffiths 1980, 167); the notion of the frontier man, as it was absorbing new types of actual people, was becoming an increasingly abstract concept, obviating its subject of concrete characteristic.

Yet, for the character to serve as an embodiment, a concrete representation of the idea—a requirement of the myth format—he had to have a set of concrete traits, to have a face and an occupation. Out of the multiplicity of what James Hall (Slotkin 1973) called a "sectional character," one had to rise to represent the nation. That abstract character had to be imaginable, recognizable, and relatable for the people, most of whom had never experienced the frontier themselves, who were separated not only in space but in time by miles and by years. The hero had to be recognizable—he had to represent a type; he had to be imaginable—he had to have unique individual traits; and he had to be relatable—he had to deal with the issues to which anyone could relate. The character also had to embody the contradictory nature of the frontier line; he could not be settled on one or the other side of it, but he would have to be constantly crossing it, belonging to both sides, and he would have to retain his quality to be forever progressing but never completed.

A search for such a character who would satisfy all the requirements and serve as the frontier hero, a carrier for the national character, was open for about a century, progressing, among other things, through literature and art; it was completed by the end of the 19th century, not without Theodore Roosevelt's coordinating and promotional input. With the closure of the physical frontier and its conversion into a myth, the frontierer, too, inevitably entered the realm of intense mythologization.

Of all the multiple characters inhabiting the frontier on both sides, of all the variety of the occupations, connections, and personal traits, a cowboy arose to the top of the competition. He had two major competitors, though. In his autobiography, Roosevelt (1913) named three major characters, who were inhabiting the "Far West, the West of Owen Wister's stories and Frederic Remington's drawings": "the buffalo-hunter, the soldier, and the cow-puncher" (Roosevelt 1913, 21). Roosevelt himself had tried on all the three roles and thus could write about them with firsthand knowledge, but there was more to this selection than simply his own experience. After all, he was also a rancher, and, probably, that part of his personal story and identity was not any smaller than that of a cowboy, yet he did not include the rancher in the cast.

In the dime novels and in the bigger literary forms too, the trio was in the first roles, and often merged in one protagonist. All three were not quite settled in the community, yet were connected to it, each in their own way. All three were crossing the frontier routinely, as a part of their duties, unlike those types, who, to cross the frontier, would have to disengage from their daily subsistence routines and do so only in response to an emergency. All three possessed professional skills required by the rough conditions of the frontier, and all three were imaginable and relatable enough to catch a ride in the collective imagination. All three, finally, were dealing with death on a regular basis, as a part of their job, claiming an archetypal depth through their bordering experiences.

Why did the cowboy, then, get ahead of the other two and secure the job of representing the national character, becoming a measure for masculinity and a metaphor for a politically potent man?

The soldier, despite unquestionably being a carrier of heroic attributes, was not an easily and positively mythologized character, suited to lead in efflorescing of the national narrative. First and foremost, the soldier did not relate to the land on either of the two sides; he related to the inhabitants on both sides: negatively to the natives on the wild side of the frontier—he fought them—and positively to the community on the civilized side—he was protecting them. The soldier was crossing the border with the goal to fight, defeat, or die. Being totally, to the point of self-denial, in the service of community, he was still an outsider to it; he was not there to stay and participate in what was coming next; he was not there to acquire social and emotional connections and settle down. With all the greatness of his sacrifice he was ready to make for the community, the soldier was only superficially related to it. If given the order, he would leave for another community to protect them, or move any place the commander would send him.

Another obstacle for the national hero obtaining the concretization in the figure of a soldier was the potential controversy of the westward advancement, its clashing meanings. The myth of the Virgin Land did not support that crucial part of an actual situation that the land, thought of as wild, was, in fact, inhabited by the aboriginal people and sacred to them. Within this context, the soldier figure was not as attractive; he could not serve as a hero in the all-national story. Given all the tragic neglect of the native people indicative of early American history (and Roosevelt's own attitude toward Native Americans), the arms turned against the native population were the arms turned to within the nation. That could not provide an image supportive of a supposedly uniting, nation-building narrative.

The hunter, like the soldier, was the frontier crosser, but, unlike the soldier, he had a closer relation to the land, which provided him with a catch and habitat. He, too, had only a superficial relation to the community, and even rare communication could, for the most part, be avoided. He walked or rode to a location of a likely prey responding to the promise of nature, having little to do with the society, and came back with the catch, only communicating with the community for an exchange of his trophy for what he needed that the wilderness could not provide. A middleman between society and the wilderness on the conditions of the latter, the hunter represented a vestigial subsistent practice no longer relevant to either reality of the socioeconomic order in formation or to the collective dream of the Jeffersonian Garden. He was the past of the nation in becoming, not its future.

The cowboy, in contrast to the soldier and the hunter, had a close relationship to both the land and the community. Stationed, unlike the hunter, on the civilized side of the divide, he was routinely, as a part of his job, going to the territories beyond the frontier line. He was crossing the line not to kill but to bring back an escaped animal, to round up a mustang, to drive cattle to a different location. He did not trade the catch; he traded his (mostly physical) skills, his labor.

The symbolic rise of the cowboy was enhanced by the natural metaphorism of the job. The daily routine of subduing the wilderness within and beyond fencing provided a perfect metaphor for frontier advancement. Breaking the horses and subduing the bulls were the cowboy's job, but more importantly, it was a symbolically meaningful action of civilizing the wildness, a dramatized and impersonated, ritualistic reproduction of the frontier in action. The fact that this drama was staged by a mixed cast of humans and, unwillingly, animals enhanced its mythological relevance. His job required skills to deal with the wilderness, live on it and from it. If the hunter pursued a wild animal to kill it, the cowboy did so to turn it from wild to domesticated; he was the one who performed that domestication, taming the wild animal just like the heroic frontierer was taming the wilderness.

Hunter and cowboy, each subordinated to natural and economic orders respectively, rather than taking orders from other people, as in the case of the soldier, embodied an opposition: the hunter represented the wilderness (capturing and killing), and the cowboy represented domestication (catching, keeping, and cultivating, killing later and on his terms). Those were two roles on the frontier divide that emphasized different sides of it, either by the nature or by the economy set order. In this scenario, the cowboy was uniquely positioned, standing with one foot on the land of the farm and with the other foot on the wild land along the frontier. He stood there like a giant, bridging the two sides with his own body, with both feet firmly on the land, owing it for the fact, yet not fixed on it by the ownership title. An abstracted individual with few specific characteristics and little if any at all property, with possessions that could all fit on the back of his horse, ready to raise and move further after and beyond the frontier line, he had nothing to anchor him in one place, little practical and no emotional attachments. The frontier land as a semi-real, abstracted place of action echoed in the cowboy as a set of several pared-down features essential for survival, making him a psychologically plain character, as mythic heroes essentially are.

The mythic cowboy was an embodied action without Inner sophistication, sharpened to deal with defined kinds of challenges. As Elliott West (1988) put it:

> The problems were simple dichotomies solved through straightforward acts taken with absolute confidence. In this sense, talk of characters' intricate motives was beside the point, for in that final, culminating moment, the hero brushed aside all complexities and settled the villain's hash.
>
> (West 1988, 76)

David Murdoch observed that the cowboy, "the last kind of hero to emerge from the frontier," was a more abstract character than all the previous heroes, "not partly but entirely a cultural artifact": "all previous frontier hero-stereotypes were epitomized in great representative individuals, but the collective American memory left the cowboy anonymous" (Murdoch 2001, 44).

One nuance seems to be important for understanding why the cowboy figure secured the role of an all-national hero. It is related to, presumably, the class arrogance of Roosevelt, who, as Richard Slotkin suggested, wrote about his "cowboy teachers" as those who worked for him mainly for the audience of the higher economic classes, "as a gentlemen-sportsman to and for others of his class" (Slotkin 1981, 615).

> While he praised the cowboys as work men and trail companions, he made it clear that he spoke and dealt with them always as the manager of the enterprise. If he worked with them, it was in order that they would work more willingly and efficiently for him.
>
> (Slotkin 1981, 615)

Slotkin attributed such an attitude to Roosevelt's belief that the progression of cultures from savagery to civilization peaked in the "Anglo-Saxon race" and, within the race, in "the most civilized and self-aware successor classes" (Slotkin 1981, 615). As Slotkin mentioned, Roosevelt admired James Fenimore Cooper, whose "aristocrat-hunting pairing" of the characters, such as an old hunter and an aristocrat, or a Virginia planter and a soldier, made it possible to affiliate class superiority with "figures symbolic of democratic belief" (Slotkin 1981, 613). In the logic of the stages of civilization, as, Slotkin speculated, Roosevelt had interpreted it, in the succession of the forms of settlement and correspondent forms of economic production, the tribal Indian hunter was inferior to and, therefore, replaced by the Anglo-Saxonian hunter, and the latter was succeeded by the cowboy, who lacked the hunter's aristocratism but, conveniently, had "no sympathy for unionism." The hunter—an "archetype of freedom"—was replaced with the cowboy—the "working hands."

The idea of upward mobility—a major point of the American Dream—can only be demonstrated as moving upward from one class to another. Those who belong to the upper class by birth and remain within that class cannot be a model for the American Dream. They can get richer, they can get well-paid or secure dream jobs, up to becoming President, but it is not what upward mobility is about because, with all the exciting progression in their lives, they would still remain within the same socioeconomic class. Bringing the cowboy—a figure of lower economic status—into the system of national mythology turned this mythologized figure into an ideological statement. The cowboy was closer to the bottom of the economic hierarchy, which gave him the room to progress, economically and socially, through his hard work and moral virtues. (To an extent, such a growth was also seen as predetermined by his natural aristocratism.) He was the right figure to become an exemplar of the American Dream, a meritocracy argument embodied in an archetypal story.

In the frontier myth, the cowboy, of course, did not grow into an owner; he remained distant from the temptations of power and comfort, but that was due to his natural asceticism and manly neglect of emotional needs: the myth said so. In other words, he was not ascending to the higher class because he did not want to do so, but he easily could if he wanted to. The cowboy's low economic status made this mythological figure serve ideological purposes better than a character of a higher economic status would; ideology must go hand in hand with national mythology to solidify its own impact. It was not merely a matter of preference that Roosevelt, who was, in fact, the owner of the ranch, not a cowboy, became the "cowboy president," not "the rancher president."

The progression of a literary character across the genres was reflective of this logic. Cooper, who introduced the frontier theme to the reading audience and started a tradition of romanticizing the American West, pictured hunter and soldier fighting with the Indians as the first line of the frontier; in a later era, when the Indian resistance was subdued, the literary frontiersmen switched to fighting immoral personalities, actions, and dangerous economic practices on the civilized side of the frontier. The dime novels, a popular read through most of the 19th century, the classic era of the westward exploration, envisioned hunters, soldiers, and outlaws as protagonists, but, eventually, the cowboy prevailed, culminating in James Steele's *The Sons of the Border* (1873) and in Owen Wisner's *The Virginian* (1902). Through the development of the dime novels, the cowboy was gradually stripped of his cattle-related job duties and turned into a fighter against the bad guys for all the good guys and girls.

The man and the towners

Ahead of others in the unknown, a hero, by definition, is the one who exceeds established margins and gives the way to a new order and a new moral structure. For the frontier man, a man of action, after he had successfully combatted the wilderness, came the task of finding his place on the civilized part of the frontier, learning to respond to the challenges within the settlement, the community. This transition was inevitable, given that the frontier was moving forward with a perspective, one day, for civilization to win and for the wilderness to be fully defeated.

In the survival mode of the frontier, the actions of the hero were restricted only by the limits of his own might, not by any rules made by another man and not by a moral code. The social order was not of concern to the hero, because his might could not be submissive to anyone's will, even the collective will. But with the wilderness retreating and the civilization advancing, a new dimension appeared in the story: ethics. Not immediate survival, but doing the right thing, acting within the established boundaries, became a criterion for the rightness of an action; the heroism and the hero could now be judged as true or not. A mighty character was now expected to measure his prospective action on a moral scale before attempting it. The hero, once holistic as an acting agency, at this stage, split in his core into his personality subject to a moral code and his action that, since it was heroic, should not be subject to any judgments. The action that was, before, an immediate reaction to the environment now became mediated by the moral judgment forced in within the hero's agency. Through this fraction, the myth propagated further into multiplying oppositions, this time between the hero's individualism and him accounting for the public good. The setting for this new development was the town.

In the border town, subordination of individualism to the social convention enabled a consensus among multiple individuals and guided in telling the good from the bad; armed with the clear rules, each member of the community was expected to stay unambiguously on the side of the good. The frontier man, though, did not always wear the white hat. As David Smith noted, "the first generation of fictional wild western heroes were primarily symbols of anarchic freedom" (Smith 2021, 81), so having to remain within the boundaries set by the morals should have been a challenge for them. Moral restrictions became not just a new challenge for the hero but a new kind of challenge, precisely one that required him to restrict his own nature, the wilderness in himself. The limits morality imposed upon the hero gave an impulse for the further development of his character, particularly his reflective side. The myth required that the new kind of heroic action, the one that had to be tested on its correspondence to moral and legal norms, had to be enacted, first, before it could be incorporated into the hero's character as his capacity for a superior moral judgment.

It was essential to the story that the hero was not a towner but was coming "from outside the society in which he operated" (Hankins 1983, 269). The hero's journey toward the town was an outer journey toward a geographic location and, at the same time, an inner journey toward himself, as formation of his inner, social core through overcoming his individualism for the public good. The cleavage of hero's inner and outer journeys enhanced the dramatic element of the story and allowed for multiple adaptations of the "business of conquering the evil" (Hankins 1983, 270)—a theme actively exploited in politics and in movies. The hero was regularly called on duty to protect the town, its people, and the order by which the people had decided to live. He was gradually reorienting himself from fighting the wilderness and having people follow him to fighting with the "wilderness" within the community, against individuals who were breaking or ignoring the norms of cohabitation. Service, not survival, became the motivation to continue the battle.

The conditioning of the hero into a lawful and moral being echoed the changes in the reputation of real cowboys who, thanks to the development of the cattle industry in the second part of the 19th century, became a numerous and distinctive type. David Murdoch provided an account of radical transformations, the "complete reverse" of the cowboy image in the public mind, first from a "ruffian," a "reckless desperado" whose "visits to the frontier towns . . . [were] regarded as a calamity second only to Western tornado" (Richard Dodge, an aide to General Sherman, as cited in Murdoch 2001, 48) to "just another figure who proved how amusingly crude an unsophisticated the West was" and, then, to a new—and final—heroic type of the frontierer. Murdoch tracked this transformation within the 20-year period starting in the mid-1880s, so the transformation had been completed by Roosevelt's first presidential campaign (and, in part, by the means of it).

The transformation of the hero was also reflected in the transition of the meaning of the "tough" from vaguely defined and ethically controversial to articulate and positive:

> "Tough" used as a noun was American invention of the 1870s, . . . its connotation was wholly unfavorable: it meant a thug or rowdy. Among heroes, too, some of America's toughest had controversial reputation." "The term itself, "tough guy," capturing in extreme form several

American notions of toughness, did not reach general currency until about 1925." "After becoming a noun, its semantics broadened: "American culture has expended formal dictionary meaning of toughness—resilience, intractability—to include mastery, competence, informal assertiveness, and self-defense.

(Wilkinson 1984, 3–7).

In the hero's glorious rebirth from an "acting being" into a "moral being," he was held back in a trap: he could not unambiguously submit to the demands of morality because, although established, the community was still threatened by the wilderness in both ways, by the wild side of the frontier and by the "wilderness" within itself—by the outlaws and other destructive characters and forces. To meet both challenges, the protector of the community had to combine both qualities—adherence to a conventional ethics and the ability to perform a heroic action. This contradiction was deep. The hero could not ignore the rules of the community because establishing the community was what he fought for at the first place; he was fighting the wilderness so that people following him to the reclaimed territories could settle down and order their lives in the manner they chose. On the other hand, he could not give up his heroic traits, for that would make him less helpful to the community than in his unrestricted might. Thus, the hero embodied the conflict of the opposite tendencies and, with it, "the conflict of ideologies between the autonomous hero and democratic equality" (Hankins 1983, 267).

Belonging to both worlds forced the hero to belong to neither. He was an impersonated wildness on the civilized side and a civilizing effort in the wildness. Standing on the divide behind the frontier line, where the laws were only those of survival, and, at the same time, on the ground of the town with its social regulations, he faced the line from both sides, mediating the turbulent relations of the wildness and the township and carrying the traits of both. The fracture of the frontier came through the man and enhanced the drama. "The hero never resolves these tensions, he lives within them," affirmed Robert Inchausti. "Various events threaten to expose him and collapse the contradictions of his life, he always escapes"; "these escapes teach us . . . how to live in two worlds" (Inchausti 1983, 66).

The idea of the hero in service to the community had at least two more underpinnings. One of them was ideological, serving a practical purpose of restraining a mighty man from his natural power, forcing him to within the regulatory limits. Another was existential. After all, when the frontier would—inevitably—disappear, the hero would have no choice but to be assimilated into the community. Reaching the end of the frontier possessed an existential threat to the hero, not as an individual, and not even as the type, but as the heroic status of the type. In other words, the existential threat for the hero was continuing existence as a man stripped of his heroic status. At that moment of existential threat to the heroic essence of the character, the community provided him with a new kind of challenge, and with that an opportunity to maintain his heroic status. From this perspective, service to the community was not only an unmercenary act, but also an act of paying back for a favor, that, in turn, brought about a balance between the service and seemingly abandoned individualism. Both challenges—that of the wilderness and that of civilization—were existential, with the difference that the first one was produced by forces external to the hero and the second one had developed withing the hero himself as a result of his choice to subordinate his freedom to service. Accepting the boundaries of the social order without giving up a heroic role was a new challenge, a rupture in the holistic character that set the premise for his eventual psychologization.

Regularly coming to the town and ready to offer his service to the community, he was still not putting roots down in the town. He did not stay there; he was leaving it as soon as his mission was achieved. He, the frontier man, had no chance to settle down, for if he did, he would "die" as the frontierer and reappear as the towner—a farmer, a lawyer, a saloon owner. A settled frontier man would vanish as a hero, and the myth would end, as would end, having hardly started, a Western, if it only pictured a settled frontier man. A settled man could only be a hero if he stood up to a challenge and become, for the duration of the movie, unsettled again. Unattached, accrete with the property and possessions, a lonely solitary figure, the hero was an archetype, not a concrete man. A concrete man, real or a protagonist, could settle, as did the Virginian; he could marry an Eastern girl, become an owner, get comfort. An archetypal figure, by contrast, could not settle down as long as the land ahead remained promising and wild, waiting for an individual not afraid of pushing the limits. Therefore, in the myth reoccurred the theme of a lonely cowboy leaving the town to return to the "desolate, stark desert" again, and again, forever.

By the time the cowboy became established as a national hero and exploited in presidential politics, the service component began to predominate over his independence and loneliness. Initially ethically ambiguous, the hero grew into a trusted, nearly absolute moral authority. The heroic character no longer remained in his pristine simplicity but moved toward acquiring relational and psychological depth.

The town served in the story as an agency, and that agency was not a character but the environment that presented a new kind of challenge to the hero and stimulated the hero's progress toward inner sophistication. The logic and the structure of myth demanded, however, that the civilized force of the town was impersonated, represented by a character. Such a character became the girl.

The girl: gendered opposition

Not least because Roosevelt and other creators of the myth "populated their stories of the West largely with men like themselves" (White 1994), masculinity was established as a key element of myth (Smith 2021, 24); the frontier experiences were recognized as primarily masculine, whereas "femininity was assigned a symbolic role of the hero's other" (Georgi-Findlay 1996, 6). A woman became a "defining opposite" for the hero (Wilkinson 1984, 8); her presence in the frontier story "was mostly to give the hero someone to protect . . . by her helplessness she emphasized the man's power and abilities" (West 1988, 74). Moreover, femininity in the frontier mythology came to represent corrupted civilization and restricting rules and, on the personal level, "obstacles to the male hero's freedom" (Georgi-Findley 1966, 6).

The frontier man, who absorbed the duality of the frontier, himself represented the opposite forces, depending on which side of the frontier divide he was at the moment. In the wilderness, he was a civilizing force, a human opposition to nature, whereas in the social world he embodied nature, wild and undomesticated principle. A woman in the hero's story impersonated a more radical civilizing agency than himself, a temptation for the hero to settle down, to ground himself on the civilized side in both its meanings: spatially, by moving to the town, and personally, by getting emotionally attached to her. The girl as a subject of the hero's emotional attachment was, in the story, not as much an agency by herself but a function of the civilizing force operating both within the hero and externally to him; she was presenting an inner challenge, an inner frontier, that provided the hero with the opportunity to move further toward psychological complexity.

As Peter Homans (1961), Jenni Calder (1974), Janice Rushing (1983), and other researchers of the Western genre observed, the duality of the hero's nature, his inner conflict, was mirrored in "splitting women into two personae, one for each aspect of the value opposition" (Rushing 1983, 15). The two girls had two distinct occupations and locations: "The brothel or dance hall is inhabited by the 'bad girl'; her counterpart, the 'good girl,' is stereotypically a schoolmarm or the rancher's daughter" (Rushing 1983, 16–17). The two girls each served a specific purpose in the story, carrying a specific symbolic load. The good girl manifested morals and a possibility, a promise of the orderly life, thus impersonated the civilizing part of the divide. She was often an Easterner, which emphasized her alienation from the West; it also demonstrated her inferiority to the Western man—a gendered power game expressed through a socio-geographic metaphor. The bad girl, on the contrast, impersonated a constant return of the hero to his primary freedom: "she does not try to make him put away his guns" (Homans 1961, 77). Enjoying some sort of hero's attachment, she was not an anchor to keep him in one place. Not demanding that the hero give up on the wild side of his contradictory essence, she was better suited for the hero practically. In a way, she served a

Theodore Roosevelt 31

transitional function in the story and was hero's own female personification. Like the hero himself, the bad girl surpassed the boundaries of morality. As such, she was sexually available outside of marriage, whereas the good girl was not; she did not require as much protection and patronizing as the good girl did; she belonged to the saloon, a controversial, frontier place within the town (West 1988), not a proper place for the good girl to visit. Settling down with the good girl would be a happy ending for a fairy tale, but such an ending would ruin the myth. As Peter Homans put it:

> To have the good girl, our hero would have to become like those depictable easterners. To get the bad girl, he would have to emulate the evil one. In such a dilemma, the ride into the sunset is not such a bad solution after all.
> (Homans 1961, 75)

Because the good girl and bad girl opposition was laid out spatially, as two specific places in the town, the brothel and the school, the hero's relations with the girl and the intensity of his emotional attachments were presented as spatial layout. The complexity of the hero, shown as a spatial opposition external to him, got internalized as the story moved forward. The land embodiment of the two-girls contradiction made it familiar for the hero to deal with, because that was what he was doing from the start: fighting the challenges presented by and on the land. Thus, in the two girls, the myth, which initially departed from its major man–land opposition, returned to the land, now enriched by the inner and relational complexity of the man. A female turned out to be more than a supportive character; she became a condition for the further development of the hero. In her duality of good and bad, the girl presented a contradiction of community and the wilderness, and, further down to the core of the myth, its major contradiction of land–man relations. The hero's relationship with the girl did both, contradicting and mirroring his relationship with the land; the land and the girl became metaphors of each other. These forces not just tore the hero apart, each pulling him to its side, but symbolically crusaded him, for he found himself torn in two dimensions—between the girl and the land and between the two girls. This conflict of equally irresistible calls preserved the structure and maintained the mythic format of the story. It also offered an opportunity to further development of the myth, because the structure of the story became more complex; it became multidimensional, offering not one, but several axes for the story to progress.

Such completion of the frontier myth settled well within the collective imagination. Land as the grand metaphor for the nation had already been around for much longer than the frontier myth and even the frontier itself. The metaphor was lent from cultural memories going back to the metropolis, to Queen Elizabeth I famously excusing herself from an unwanted marriage by claiming her marriage to England. In the new, American version of the metaphor, the relation was reversed from a "virgin" woman married to her kingdom to the man staying in complicated relationships with the "virgin" land. The East–West, metropolis–colony, civilization–wildness, corruption–purity oppositions were gendered and embodied in those relationships. They also contained a reversed social conflict: if the queen was at the very top of the social hierarchy and owned the land by her inborn right, the American frontier man was on the opposite side of the social hierarchy and had to fight his way up and subjugate "no one's" land. The queen possessed the land, owned it, while the frontier man was chasing after it, attacking and protecting it at the same time but never truly holding it in his hands, never owning it; the land remained virgin for as long as he remained a hero. The queen was symbolically married to the kingdom at the moment of her coronation, not as her choice, but in an act of fulfilling her duty; the cowboy was in relationship with the land by his choice, but never "married," always battling and conquering. For Elizabeth, England—her land—was her husband, and her subjects were her children; for the cowboy, the land was his earthly and heavenly love, a conquered lover and an unreachable desire. In a way, it was for him a metaphor of a woman in both major archetypal hypostases, a mistress and a mother (Kolodny 1975). The coronation ring as a sign of the royal marriage of the monarch to the land she ruled was transformed into the ring broken and unfolded into the straight line of the frontier, visualizing the colony breaking its ties with the metropolis. Rupert Wilkinson (1984, 119) tracked this metaphor, paralleling the isolation of the frontier line and the loneliness of the "individualistic man of the West," of "an isolate and unmarried male figure" (Kolodny 1975, 135). Faithful to the land, called by the land, the hero returned there every night, forever wanting and never truly getting what he most wanted and what was the birthplace of him as a hero.

This metaphoric drama of projecting femininity upon the Western landscape (see: Kolodny 1975, 1984) resurfaced in the story of Theodore Roosevelt, who responded to the call of the Western territories after losing, in one day, both his most beloved women: his wife and his mother. Of course, fresh air and busy life on a ranch in Wyoming created a perfect antidote to grief, but the healing power of the Western lands was also metaphorically charged. Who and what kind of relations he lost, he found a resemblance of in the spatial and symbolic arrangements of the West.

The Lacanian fold, the merge through repulsion of the royal and cowboy figures in their relation to the land, contributed to establishing the cowboy as a legitimate, all-national hero, infusing him with royalty, aristocratism, and entitlement. The bifurcated female character completed the archetypal layout of the frontier story by returning it to the initial land–man opposition. It was logical that the hero's relation with land ended up being presented through gendered metaphors of archetypal scale. Whether a mother or a mistress, embracing or expelling, land summoned the cowboy with an eternal appeal; and in response, overpowering her resistance and seeking her acceptance, he offered his masculinity—forthright, stirring, hypertrophied—to match her divine scale. Did he, a mortal man, have a chance to measure up to the divine femininity without overly exaggerating his manly traits? Probably not. He had to present himself in these relationships in an equally mythic proportion and, in opposition to her supreme femininity, as a mighty, victorious, excessive masculinity.

References

Binkovitz, Leah. 2013. "Who Were the Six Native American Chiefs in Teddy Roosevelt's Inaugural Parade?" *Smithsonian Magazine*, January 16.

Bowden, Martyn J. 1992. "The Invention of American Tradition." *Journal of Historical Geography* 18 (1): 3–26.

Calder, Jenni. 1974. *There Must Be a Lone Ranger*. London: Hamish Hamilton Ltd.

Doniger, Wendy. 1995. "Foreword." In *Myth and Meaning: Cracking the Code of Culture*, edited by Claude Lévi-Strauss, vii–xv. New York: Schocken Books.

The Editors of Encyclopedia Britannica. 2023. "World's Columbian Exposition." In *Encyclopedia Britannica*, January 27. Accessed February 13, 2023. www.britannica.com/event/Worlds-Columbian-Exposition.

Erikson, Erik. 1993. *Childhood and Society*. 2nd ed. New York: W. W. Norton & Company.

Fees, Paul. n.d. "Wild West Shows: Buffalo Bill's Wild West." *Buffalo Bill Center of the West*. https://centerofthewest.org/learn/western-essays/wild-west-shows/.

Georgi-Findlay, B. 1996. *The Frontiers of Women's Writing: Women's Narratives and the Rhetoric of Westward Expansion*. Tucson: The University of Arizona Press.

Georgi-Findlay, Brigitte. 1996. *Women's Narratives and the Rhetoric of the Western Expansion*. Tucson: The University of Arizona Press.

Goetzmann, William H. and William N. Goetzmann. 1986. *The West of the Imagination*. New York: W. W. Norton & Company.

Griffiths, John, C. 1980. *Three Tomorrows: American, British, and Soviet Science Fiction*. Totowa, N. J.: Barnes & Noble Books.

Hall, James. 1828. *Letters from the West: Containing Sketches of Scenery, Manners, and Customs*. London: Henry Colburn. Google Books. https://bit.ly/3EEx8H5.

Hankins, Sarah. 1983. "Archetypal Alloy: Reagan's Rhetorical Image." *Central States Speech Journal* 34 (1): 33–43. doi:10.1080/10510978309368112.

Hauss, Miriam. 2004. "An Etching for the AHA." *Perspectives on History*. https://bit.ly/3F2LNND.

Homans, Peter. 1961. "Puritanism Revisited: An Analysis of the Contemporary Screen-Image Western." *Studies in Public Communication* 3: 73–84.

Inchausti, Robert. 1983. "The Superhero's Two Worlds." In *The Hero in Transition*, edited by Ray B. Browne and Marshall W. Fishwick, Bowling Green, Ohio: Bowling Green University Popular Press. Pp. 66–83.

Kolodny, Annette. 1975. *The Lay of the Land: Metaphor as Experience and History in American Life and Letters*. Chapel Hill: University of North Carolina Press.

———. 1984. *The Land Before Her: Fantasy and the Experience of the American Frontiers, 1830–1860*. Chapel Hill: The University of North Carolina Press.

Library of Congress. n.d. "The Log Cabin Campaign of 1840." *American History from American Library*. www.americaslibrary.gov/aa/harrison/aa_harrison_whharrison_2.html.

Lofaro, Michael. n.d. "David Crockett." In *The Handbook of Texas Online*. Accessed October 17, 2022. www.sonsofdewittcolony.org/adp/history/bios/crockett/crockett.html.

Murdoch, David H. 2001. *The American West: The Invention of Myth*. Cardiff: Welsh Academic Press.

Rogin, Michael P. 1987. *Ronald Reagan the Movie: And Other Episodes of Political Demonology*. Berkeley, Los Angeles and London: University of California Press.

———. 1899. "Theodore Roosevelt to John Tanner." Illinois State Archive, Governor Record Series 101.023, John Riley Tanner Correspondence, March 25.

———. 1913. *Theodore Roosevelt; an Autobiography*. New York: The Macmillan Company.

Rushing, Janice Hocker. 1983. "The Rhetoric of the American Western Myth." *Communication Monographs* 50 (1): 14–32. https://doi.org/10.1080/03637758309390151.

Slotkin, Richard. 1973. *Regeneration Through Violence: The Mythology of the American Frontier, 1600–1860*. Middleton: Wesleyan University Press.

———. 1981. "Nostalgia and Progress: Theodore Roosevelt's Myth of the Frontier." *American Quarterly* 33 (5): 608–37. www.ezproxy.shsu.edu/10.2307/2712805.

———. 1985. *The Fatal Environment: The Myth of the Frontier in the Age of Industrialization, 1800–1890*. New York: Atheneum.

Smith, David. 2021. *Cowboy Presidents: The Frontier Politics and US Myth Since 1990*. Norman, OK: University of Oklahoma Press.

Steele, James W. 1873. *The Sons of the Border. Sketches of the Life and People on the Far Frontier*. Common Wealth Printing Company.

Turner, Frederick. 1966. *The Significance of the Frontier in American History*. New York: Continuum.

West, Elliott. 1988. "Shots in the Dark: Television and the Western Myth." *Montana: The Magazine of Western History* 38 (2): 72–76. www.jstor.org/stable/4519136.

———. 1996. *The Saloon on the Rocky Mountain Mining Frontier*. London: University of Nebraska Press.

White, Richard. 1994. "Frederick Jackson Turner and Buffalo Bill." In *The Frontier in American Culture*, edited by Richard White, Patricia Nelson Limerick, and James R. Grossman, 7–65. Berkeley, Los Angeles and London: University of California Press.

The White House. n.d. "William Henry Harrison." *The White House*. Accessed November 1, 2022. https://georgewbush-whitehouse.archives.gov/history/presidents/wh9.html.

Wilkinson, Rupert. 1984. *American Tough: The Tough Guy Tradition and American Character*. New York, Cambridge, Philadelphia, San Francisco, London, Mexico City, Sao Paolo, Singapore and Sydney: Perennial Library.

Wright, Will. 1975. *Six Guns and Society: A Structural Study of the Western*. Berkeley, Los Angeles and London: University of California Press.

3 Ronald Reagan

Extension of the frontier and inversion of the hero

Myth gains primacy

When Ronald Reagan took the Oval Office for his two-term presidency, the reality of the frontier was so long gone that it could hardly provide any basis for promoting a presidential image. The frontier story, on the contrary, was elaborated in details and a multiplicity of plots, by the 1980s nestling firmly in popular culture, primarily in the motion picture. Upgraded with Hollywood-supplied visualizations and sound, it created a more intimate connection with the Western stories and characters than shading away, with the gone generations, recollections about the wild West. Played out on the screen, the drama of the frontier became an immediate experience for the public, and on cinematic grounds, the bygone frontier reappeared as a more persuasive reality than the reality itself.

Ronald Reagan came to politics with a collection of Hollywood-produced characters and the baggage of the screen-borrowed heroic virtues under his belt. His background as an actor, a radio commentator, and a corporate front man made him a good candidate for giving the myth a new, potent momentum: the electorate, on whose attachment to the frontier theme he could capitalize, the electorate, who 80 years earlier were the dime-novel readers, were now the movie watchers. In the collective imagination of the second part of the 20th century, the presidential image of Reagan was developed, synchronized, and universalized by cinematic art as an embodiment of a heroic type who possessed the virtues requested from the leader of the nation, including the "pristine sense of right and wrong" (Murdoch 2001).

"Reagan was selling an image, a rehearsal product" (Hankins 1983, 267), deriving "much of his image from the movies" and trying "to use them to further his political aims" (Tolchin 1985). The screen version of Reagan-the-Westerner wore a white Stetson as a sign of a gift of exceptional moral judgment and adherence to the public service (in more than 50 movies Reagan starred, he played a villain only once); this heroic image was loaded with an ideological agenda and appropriated for political purposes (Smith 2021, 212). The image of Reagan overshadowed the political agenda he was delivering,

DOI: 10.4324/9781003415312-3

and it covered for the massive disapproval of that agenda among Americans. It was the image, not the agenda, that was so much appreciated by numerous accounts of Reagan's masterful delivery of the presidential message. As David Smith (2021) reminded us, Reagan's presidential image, paradoxically, was enhanced in popularity after Reagan left the office.

Reagan's reputation as "the great communicator," "by far the most persuasive political speaker of our times" (Erikson 1985, 1) was boosted by constant references to his cinematic presence and by regular reuse of the lines he borrowed from the movies he starred in. Some lines were literal borrowings, others were rephrasing or referencing. "Where is the rest of me?" "I am paying for this microphone!" "Where do we find such men?" "Win one for the Gipper!" He was turning those lines, crafted by collective efforts of moviemaking teams and tried against the tastes of the audiences, into cinematic metaphors, a myth-creating engine.

Reagan not just spoke by the lines from the films in which he starred, but he rode big time on them. His 1980 presidential campaign slogan "Let's make America great again" resembled a line from a classic trailer to the 1940 movie "Santa Fe Trail": "The fighting heroes who made America great" (Rotten Tomatoes 2014), where Reagan played one of the supporting roles. The variations of the phrase were used in politics before, but reference to the movie was likely a more influential source of inspiration for Reagan or, rather, his PR team. The catchphrase, then, migrated to Bill Clinton's 1992 presidential campaign slogan "Together we can make America work again" and, after being exploited on a smaller scale by some other politicians, finally, settled down on the MAGA hats of Donald Trump's supporters.

Notably merged with his cinematic roles, Reagan viewed doing politics as similar to acting in films (Rogin 1987, 17). He described his first political address at a students' meeting on a college campus back in 1964, in theatrical terms: "I discovered that night that an audience has a feel to it and that, in the parlance of the theater, that audience and I were together" (Erikson 1985, 13). Paul Erikson (ibid.) commented on this reflection: "Reagan characterized his listeners as the audience, and himself as an actor, who used words to go beyond conveying ideas to achieving a subliminal identification." Erikson noted Reagan's 1981 farewell Californian speech before his departure to Washington, DC for the inauguration as an example of exceptional storytelling craftmanship: "We see in President Reagan's short parable all the standard elements of fiction" (Erikson 1985, 51–52). In his political speeches, Reagan created a stock of characters that included heroes and villains (ibid.) and masterfully performed the obliteration of the reality specific for myth (Rogin 1987). Rogin illustrated the latter with Reagan's 1986 address on military aid to Nicaragua: as Reagan spoke and the "words and pictures brought his Nicaragua into American living rooms, the real Latin American country disappeared" (ibid., xvi).

For Reagan, a career actor and a holder of a remarkable imagination (as a radio commentator, he was able to make up his commentaries without seeing an actual game), it was convenient and natural to comprehend and present the politics through cinematic metaphors. They revoked sentiments of his own past, success, fame, and attractiveness of the heroic self-presentation. "Ronald Reagan found out who he was by whom he played on film," wrote Rogin (ibid.); by "mixing political present with cinematic past" (CBS Evening News 1988), "Reagan merged his on-screen and off-screen identities" and created "the confusion between life and film . . . , the image that has fixed our gaze" (Rogin 1987, 3, 5).

Many of the movie lines Reagan reused in his addresses were references to myths of the Wild West and its characters. "Win one for the Gipper!", one of Reagan's signature lines, strangely echoed the "signature line" of Buffalo Bill Cody: "The first scalp for Custer!"—words with which Cody, then a scout in the ranks of the 5th Cavalry Regiment, displayed the scalp of an Indian warrior he had defeated and scalped. Cody himself made this episode widely known by actively sharing it with the press and exploited its dramatic appeal in the Wild West Show, where he staged the "Custer's Last Stand" moment of the Battle of Warbonnet Creek as the culmination scene. The theme of revenge for a stricken comrade, victory after a bitter defeat, a collective stand for a killed or impaired member of the group, invested the story with romanticism and heroism, though with little regard to the real meaning of the initial event.

By "dissolving the boundaries between film and real life," by spinning up the transformation between cinematic and real worlds to the point of their convergence, Reagan, like Roosevelt, exploited the boundary confusion—a concept Michael Rogin offered for describing the mechanisms of the impact of Reagan's speech. One of the illustrations Rogin used to demonstrate the boundary confusion concept was a famous episode from the 1981 Academy Awards. The night before the event, Reagan had survived an assassination attempt, and his address to the Academy audience was broadcast from his hospital bed.

> "Movies are forever" was the theme of the 1981 Academy Awards. President Ronald Reagan, the first Hollywood actor elevated to the presidency, was scheduled to welcome the Academy from the White House. "Film is forever," the President was to tell the Academy. . . . As confirming evidence of the power of myth, John W. Hinckley, imitating the plot of the movie *Taxi Driver*, deliberately shot the president on the day of the Academy award. . . . . Millions of Americans experienced the assassination attempt by watching it over and over again on television. The power of the film image confirmed the shooting, it also allowed Reagan to speak to the Academy the next night. . . . The television audience watching a screen saw a Hollywood audience watch another screen. One audience saw the other applaud a tapped image of a healthy Reagan while the real president lay in a hospital bed.
>
> (Rogin 1987, 3–4)

Another illustration of boundary confusion and cross-referencing of reality and performance was "the climax of the 1984 Republican National Convention in Dallas," where,

> in a tribute to Nancy Reagan, the convention showed film clips . . . in which both she and Mr. Reagan played. . . . When Mrs. Reagan addressed the convention after the film clips, she urged the delegates: "Make it one more for the Gipper." Watching his wife, with her arms raised, on a television screen from their hotel suite, the President waved back, and that was shown, too.
>
> (Tolchin 1985)

Presenting political issues through cinematic metaphors, so natural for Reagan, came handy for influencing the public, whose responsiveness to cinematic representations had already been fertilized by televised entertainment in general, and by the Hollywood-produced Westerns in particular. What would require an extended presentation and justification as a political statement could be succinctly and more effectively communicated through a cinematic proxy. Near and dear to the minds and hearts of the audience, metaphoric format allowed them to shift their attention and perceptions from the potentially problematic meanings of political agendas to those of a televised event. In his speeches, Reagan transmitted to the public messages coded with cinematic associations that were as much about the politics as they were about watching the movies, and since the movie-produced, myth-induced images were primary to the public's perception, they became more than merely vehicles for delivering ideological agenda—they facilitated an absorption of that agenda without clearing it from the metaphor-induced meanings and without questioning the relevance of the metaphor. Political and ideological substances were replaced by cinematic metaphorism, the boundary confusions in the non-stop turnaround between the screen and the reality eliminated the criteria of what was real and what was not, the electorate was redefined into an audience—those developments took the myth creating process to a new level and recharged the revision of both, the qualities of the hero and the major contradiction of the frontier myth—the hero's relation with the land.

The exhauster of myth

On the presidential position, the hero became the center of social connections, a head of the system of institutions, a public figure. His traits had to be adjusted to his new status. Some of the key features, such as being disconnected, independent, lonely, and short-spoken, did not suit the presidential image organically. Instead of retreating into the sunset after completing his task, the hero was now expected to retreat to his chair in the Oval Office and continue taking care of public businesses. After the work for the day was completed, he still could not escape to the wilderness, but only to the private rooms of the White House to spend the scarce hours of leisure with his family. The hero was now deemed to stay "in the town," in the house always on display (was it Michelle Obama, who compared living in the White House to living in an aquarium, a seeing-through place, a pilgrimage destination?) And even outside the White House, the hero-president could not get away from being the center of attention, because the whole country was now his town to protect, and the whole nation was the community to serve.

The necessity to sacrifice with his loneliness and freedom came with compensation, though. Initially exempted from the socioeconomic system or, as a cowboy, being close to the bottom of it, the hero-president found himself on the top of the social hierarchy. The myth had already legitimized him as an individual of exceptional qualities, so occupying the highest position seemed natural, and that evoked associations with the highest secular power—a sovereign, a ruler, whose superior status would be fixed by his birth right. For a president, the sovereign status was metaphorical, but due to the central role of metaphor in overall construction of the presidential image, the fact that exceptionality was metaphoric did not lessen its value. Since the heroic features were initially defined by relations of the man with the land, it was natural for the man, who progressed to the highest status, also to be land-bound.

In his analysis of Reagan's manner to present himself, Michael Rogin (1987) appealed to the doctrine of the king's two bodies as applied to American presidency. According to the doctrine, the corporeal body of the king and the entity of his subjects, the so-called "body politic," constitute metaphors for each other. Rogin observed that Reagan implemented this doctrine by merging, in his speeches, his own physical body with the body of the nation. Rogin demonstrated this pattern through the 1981 Academy Awards ceremony speech, cited earlier with regard to boundary confusion. Reagan spoke to the public from his clinic bed: "Thanks to some very fine people, my health is much improved. I'd like to be able to say that with regard to the health of the economy" (Rogin 1987, 4). Thus, by equating his personal recovery with the economic recovery of the nation, Reagan "was employing a very old symbolism, one that merges the body of a political leader and the body of his realm" (ibid., 5). Moreover, "he was presenting himself as the healer, laying his hands on the sick social body" (ibid., 5). Rogin reminded that Reagan was not a pioneer in utilizing the king's two bodies doctrine, that monarchs and later political leaders often "reabsorb that mystic community into their own personal bodies" (ibid., 5). Richard Slotkin observed a similar tactic used by Roosevelt, who "projected his personal psychology onto public affairs . . . equated his own early struggles against physical weakness with his country's rise to power" (Slotkin 1981, 614). The king's two-bodies doctrine turned out to be persistent in presidential imagery, for we can find it in Donald Trump's speeches as well. Like Roosevelt and Reagan, Trump routinely identifies himself with the nation, for instance by making parallels between his own financial situation and that of the country: "Who knows better about hard times than me? I had a company, it was doing well, I had tremendous debt like this country, and in 1990 the whole country just went very very bad" (NBC News 2016).

The construction of president as a "king body" meant the merging of national and biographical discourses, of public and private histories (Rogin 1987, xvii), of the political and personal symbolism. By loosening the boundaries of social and personal, Reagan infused the cowboy figure with the meanings of the supreme power—a radical improvement in the cowboy's career but not the final destination in his symbolic upward mobility. The sovereign of the land was the climax position within the social hierarchy, but there was still room to go beyond that, up along the vertical axis, beyond the social into the transcendental realm, and Reagan moved his presidential image further up. It was a natural development within the king's two-bodies conceptual frame because this doctrine is firmly connoted with the concept of two bodies of Christ (Kantorowicz 1957; Rogin 1987). By long-established associations within Christian culture, a shepherd (not quite a cowboy, but good enough as a substitute), the king, and God are merged in the figure of the Lord, the ruler of the people—his flock. To enhance the opulence of his presidential image, Reagan exploited this metaphoric trinity and appropriated the entire range of statuses by crossing the boundaries between the sacred and the profane and connecting the two realms.

Indicative in this respect were Reagan's remarks at the opening of "The American Cowboy" exhibit at the Library of Congress in 1983. With his usual charm, Reagan thanked the organizers of the exhibition for helping Washington to "get to know the American cowboy again . . . to get some sorely needed horse sense" (Reagan 1983a). He opened his remarks with an immediate reference to a movie in which he starred: "We have just had a tour of the exhibit, and as we went along, I kept looking and looking for something from *Cattle Queen of Montana.*' [Laughter] I wasn't the cattle queen—Barbara Stanwyck was. [Laughter]" (ibid.). This was a delicate, covert self-reference to himself as a king, given that by the part, Reagan's protagonist was a protector and a prospective husband of the "cattle queen." "And I did one called 'Cowboy,'" he added.

In the *Cattle Queen of Montana*, a 1952 movie recognized by critics as mediocre and probably still remembered because of Reagan's special affection for it, the protagonist was a secretly embedded government man with a cover story of being a frontier gunman. The protagonist, usually low-profile, took on the leadership in critical situations; in a culmination fight scene, he told the "queen": "Remember as I told you to keep your head down." He said that during a shooting episode, meaning that she had to hide from the bullets, but the wording opened the floor to metaphorical interpretations; it carried connotations of an experienced warrior patronizing a woman, and not an ordinary woman, but a "queen," no matter how peculiar the world she ruled was. She was, in the movie plot, armed and skilled enough to stand up for herself, but with the arrival of the hero, she was immediately put in the position of one who needed protection and was granted it in a patronizing manner. The power structure that Reagan evoked, in this speech, by bringing over the *Cattle Queen* association, was as follows: the cattle on the bottom—"a very good society, born and bred in the wide-open spaces" (ibid.), then, higher up, the queen of the cattle, and then, on the very top, himself—the savior, the protector, the cattle king, who orders the queen to keep her head down (for her safety, indeed) and demonstrates a "strong stewardship to lead the flock" (Rushing 1983, 20).

Before the speech, the Librarian of Congress, Daniel J. Boorstin, presented the Reagans with bandanas that were "a precise copy of a campaign bandana for Theodore Roosevelt, who had the distinction of being not only one of our best presidents, but to be known and the cowboy president" (Reagan 1983a). Whether Boorstin meant to make a connection between Roosevelt and Reagan as cowboy presidents or he just presented something relevant to the theme of the exhibition item is unclear—after all, the statue of James Madison in James Madison Memorial Hall, where the reception took place, also wore a bandana, although not of that historic design, and neither James Madison nor his statue had much to do with cowboyhood. The connection was made, however, by the spirit of Reagan's remarks, positioning him as another, and the only cowboy president after Roosevelt. Reagan did mention Dwight Eisenhower as "another president from the West," implying himself to be from the West as well, for he named no other presidents before naming Eisenhower. He talked about his own "fondness for Western art" and his continuing efforts to bring the Western influences to Washington, DC.

That was a deliberate twist. A Kansas native, Eisenhower was, indeed, a Westerner (he even presented a Western-style treat to the crowd by being lassoed during his inauguration), whereas neither Reagan nor Roosevelt were. The fact that two Easterners—a wealthy Harvard graduate from New York and a Hollywood actor raised in Illinois and nicknamed "Dutch"—acquired the title of cowboy presidents did not delegitimize their status, as Reagan quoted a "noted historian" (whoever that "noted historian" was and whether there was one at all): "Americans, in making their Western myths, were not put off by discrepancies with reality. Americans believed about the West not so much what was true, but what they thought ought to be true'" (ibid.). The eastern origin of many "Western" creators of the myth and politicians was rather a rule than an exception.

While extending the presidential image from the cowboy (-president) to a sovereign of the land and, further, to the Lord, Reagan repeatedly presented himself as a binding agency between the nation and an ordinary individual American. He did so by remaining—in his speeches—rooted at the lowest step of the hierarchy as a symbolic cowboy but also by emphasizing his humbleness, as well as by using an intimate tone, the one that a guru of hostage negotiation, Chriss Voss, called "the late-night FM DJ voice"—a low, breathy voice as smiling or otherwise demonstrating empathy. With his masterfully crafted and just as masterfully delivered narratives, with his presence on the big and small screen of the cinema theaters and TV sets in the living rooms of American families, Reagan kept the symbolic line between himself and the general public, the "ordinary man" as fluid and permeable, as it was between the reality and the stories he told. On the eve of his election, he was asked: "What is it, governor, that people see in you?" and he responded: "Would you laugh if I told you that they look at me and they see themselves?" (American Experience: Reagan 2020). With Reagan speaking, whoever agreed to take a ride with him to the world constructed by his performance was carrying on the hero's armor, polished by Reagan to a shine.

The expansion of the spectrum of the hero's social (to the king) and existential (to the divine) statuses brought about a change in his relations with the land. It was not accidental that land-related metaphors recurred in Reagan's speeches again and again. Likewise, in his welcome speech to the country music performers at the White House, he called Washington, DC "this land of ours," meaning the overly politicized East as opposed to the remaining traditional and pure West that his guests supposedly represented (Reagan 1983b). Each of the three statuses—the cowboy, the sovereign, and the Lord—implied a specific relation between the land and the hero, but the general pattern was that as the hero was traveling upward the hierarchy, his immediate connection with the land as the source of the challenge and a condition of his heroic status was weakening. At the bottom of the hierarchy, the man worked the land, slept on the land, and lived off the land; he related to the land by using his own, mostly physical, skills. The sovereign's relation with the land was mediated by the will of the Lord—from above, and by the skills of those who worked the land—from below. The sovereign owned the land, but the owned land, in turn, defined him and "owned" him; he was fixed to his land not by his skills, but by blood, by birth, by anointment. The Lord defined the anointed, their lands, and their subjects; moreover, He created the land and defined its attributes. Incorporation of the meanings of a sovereign and the Lord allowed the hero to move from the initial dependency of his own heroic qualities upon the land (as a man) to owning the land and defining the order for the subjects (as a sovereign), and further up to the point where he defined the land ontologically and in it predicates (as the Lord).

Reagan exploited all the three incarnations, combining them in one act and rooting the hero in both directions, as natural on the bottom side of the axis and as divine on the upper side of it. This allowed Reagan to make a major progression in the hero character by infusing him with the maximum of power in all three domains, natural, secular, and sacred. He also removed the remaining limitations that the reality placed upon the character and opened the character and the land to unrestricted fantasy. The limitations placed upon the story by the reality of the frontier completely vanished, as did the limitations placed by any kind of reality upon the development of the story. Not just geographic and historical, but any spatial and temporal limitations in the story of the frontier were removed; the frontier was now free to extend beyond any imaginable limits, and it moved so far away that it became beyond imaginable.

A cinematic metaphor arrived on time. The *Star Wars* saga became a perfect replica of the classic Western and offered an unlimited space for further advancement of the myth and the hero. *Star Wars* provided a visualization and a sound to the frontier of the frontiers, the meta-frontier. The unlimited "spaces" allowed the hero to expand his heroism in both directions, by going skyward to the faraway galaxies and by immersing himself in the archetypal depths. The hero, who in the initial version of the frontier myth was devoid of psychological complexity, now presented inner sophistication, even though his sophistication was predefined by the structure of the archetype, not by his individuality. In other words, the psychological complexity and attraction of the hero (in the case of the *Star Wars* impersonated in Luke Skywalker) came not from his personality—not quite yet—but from his virgin spiritual transparency, through which the archetype presented itself. Moreover, the spatial and temporal travel of the hero became only an external, inessential part of his real, inner travel, his growth as a person and as an independent actor—as an agency, now enriched with complexity, and as the might enhanced by the challenges of a cosmic scale.

In this new layout of spatial and psychological meta-frontier, the final point could never be reached; the journey could never end. Not only the highs (cosmic) and the depths (archetypal) of the expansion were unreachable and, by definition, unlimited; if at any point one of the two lines of the story was exhausted, the story could switch itself to the other dimension and thus move forward, fueling the inner journey with events of the external struggle and vice versa. This feature of the extended myth has been massively exploited by the movie industry, offering unlimited opportunities to retell the same myth again and again.

There was a catch, though, in unlocking the myth to unlimited interpretations of its basic format, and it was that the story itself reached its logical limit. The story could be endlessly retold through modification of its details, but it was not developing in its essence; the hero remained at the abstracted format of an archetype—a feature that was adding depth and universality to the story but was leaving the individuality of the hero blurred and restricted. Despite the multiplicities of possible variations of the same story, the myth was essentially completed. Its source, its moving force—the opposition of land and man—was reversed. The land was no longer defining the hero's features, but the hero accumulated enough power to overcome any challenges at all; there were no more challenges that would contribute to further growth of his might—it was already unlimited. From now on, the hero himself was defining the frontier, its location in space and time, and the character of the challenges he was willing to face; the frontier was now where the hero was placing it; frontier became a function of the hero. Not the qualities of the land, but the virtues of the mature hero became the moving force of the story. In fact, there was no more need in the land at all for the myth to continue; the challenge could now come only from within the hero himself or from another character, who would be in a special relation to the hero.

A challenge coming from the hero himself would make a good story, but it would not be a myth, because the myth format dictates the inner complexity to be outsourced to another character. That other character would have to be of a similar scale of might but with the opposite qualities, he would have to embody all and everything against which the white-Stetson-hat hero stood.

The entrance of a villain was prepared, but the moment was not a good for him to enter the stage quite yet. The Cold War ended with the dissolution of the major threat, "The Evil Empire," as Reagan referenced the USSR, so there was still time before the heroic showdown of Good and Evil became a political necessity again. And the persona of the villain was yet to be cast. None of the latest Soviet or post-Soviet leaders was a good fit for the newly created role anyway. But, most importantly, there was one more, last transformation for the American hero to go through, and one more direction for the myth to expand in. That is where Donald Trump entered the stage.

References

American Experience: Reagan. 2020. "From the Collection: The Presidents." *PBS*, August 11. www.pbs.org/wgbh/americanexperience/films/reagan/.

CBS Evening News. 1988. "Ronald 'The Gipper' Reagan." *CBS Evening News*, March 9. Accessed March 31, 2019. www.youtube.com/watch?v=bgg6OblbO_A.

Erikson, Paul. 1985. *Reagan Speaks*. New York: New York University Press.

Hankins, Sarah. 1983. "Archetypal Alloy: Reagan's Rhetorical Image." *Central States Speech Journal* 34 (1): 33–43. doi:10.1080/10510978309368112.

Kantorowicz, Ernst. 1957. *The King's Two Bodies: A Study in Medieval Political Theology*. Princeton and Oxford: Princeton University Press.

Murdoch, David H. 2001. *The American West: The Invention of Myth*. Cardiff: Welsh Academic Press.

NBC News. 2016. "1980s: How Donald Trump Created Donald Trump." *NBC News*, Filmed video 4:51, July. www.youtube.com/watch?v=_FLo14GMYos.

Reagan, Ronald. 1983a. "President Reagan's Remarks at the Opening of 'The American Cowboy' Exhibit." Filmed at the Library of Congress, Washington, DC, March 24. Accessed January 26, 2017. www.youtube.com/watch?v=L_n7IG0sFUc.

———. 1983b. "Remarks at a Rodeo of the Professional Rodeo Cowboy Association in Landover, Maryland." Ronald Reagan Presidential Library and Museum, September 24. www.reaganlibrary.gov/archives/speech/remarks-rodeo-professional-rodeo-cowboy-association-landover-maryland.

Rogin, Michael P. 1987. *Ronald Reagan the Movie: And Other Episodes of Political Demonology*. Berkeley, Los Angeles and London: University of California Press.

Rotten Tomatoes Classic Trailers. 2014. "Santa Fe Trail (1940) Official Trailer—Errol Flynn, Ronald Reagan Western Movie HD." Filmed 1940. @RottenTomatoes-CLASSICTRAILERS, video 2:11. www.youtube.com/watch?v=SposGx8dZts.
Rushing, Janice Hocker. 1983. "The Rhetoric of the American Western Myth." *Communication Monographs* 50 (1): 14–32. doi:10.1080/03637758309390151.
Slotkin, Richard. 1981. "Nostalgia and Progress: Theodore Roosevelt's Myth of the Frontier." *American Quarterly* 33 (5): 608–37. www.ezproxy.shsu.edu/10.2307/2712805.
Smith, David. 2021. *Cowboy Presidents: The Frontier Politics and US Myth Since 1990*. Norman, OK: University of Oklahoma Press.
Tolchin, Martin. 1985. "How Reagan Always Gets the Best Lines." *The New York Times*, September 9. www.nytimes.com/1985/09/09/us/how-reagan-always-gets-the-best-lines.html.

4 Donald Trump
Recovered meanings of the frontier and resurgence of the hero

Back to the beginning

Well discussed have been multiple references of Trump's presidential image to that of Reagan and similarities between the two men. Both were Easterners who yet acquired a place in the Western myth; both were outsiders to the political establishment; politics was the second career path for both; both, at some point, switched their political affiliation from Democrat to Republican; and both were television personalities before they ran for the office, to name a few. And, of course, they shared a one-word apart slogan: of Reagan's presidential campaign of 1976 "Let's make America great again" and Trump's 2016 MAGA ("Make American Great Again").

Such a close referencing was possible because, among other factors, Reagan and Trump impersonated two sequent stages in the development of the frontier myth. After Reagan had pushed the frontier myth to its limits, a niche for exploiting it in politics drastically narrowed. The way to maintain its vividness was to reclaim its initial, forgotten meanings, to re-root the myth back in the reality. Trump became a nearly ideal candidate to perform that task.

It is hard to imagine a figure more alien to the Western scenery than Donald Trump. A New Yorker living in a three-story Louis XIV–style penthouse on top of a skyscraper, a partygoer, and a connoisseur of women's charms, he wears a tweed haute couture coat, and the closest he gets to nature and fitness is probably walking the polished greenery of the golf course. It is almost ironic that as remote as possible from the cowboy style character as Donald Trump happened to take a leading part in a further development of the myth with the cowboy hero in the heart of it. To see why Trump turned out to be a suitable candidate for this role, we need to take a step back and examine the pool of the meanings of the frontier, to see what unexploited reserves might remain there that could help revitalize the exhausted myth and give it a new developmental impulse.

In his fundamental account of the American frontier (1973, 1981, 1985, 1992), Richard Slotkin suggested that some of the original meanings of the frontier did not make it into its mythologized story. Those meanings happened

DOI: 10.4324/9781003415312-4

to be essential to the formation of the actual frontier, but they received little articulation in the story of it because the academic accounts of the Western expansion aligned with myth, not with the reality. As Slotkin put it, the frontier theory "masks what it seems to explain" (Slotkin 1985, 45).

Slotkin argued that the frontier substantiated primarily as a socioeconomic phenomenon, and the forces that brought it into existence in the first place (and the meanings of which did not make it to the myth) were those of production. Slotkin appointed three conditions that started the economic engine of the frontier: land to explore, capital to invest, and labor to perform the work. The combination of these three conditions made what Slotkin called three types of the frontier.

The first type (Slotkin called it the resources frontier) was "represented by cheap, abundant, arable land" and its mineral wealth. The abundancy, however, "depended upon the availability of capital and labor to explore it. . . . The cheap land Frontier of the West . . . was matched by a 'cheap labor' Frontier of the East" (ibid., 45–46). This is why the second type, Slotkin argued, was the labor frontier, a "labor pool of industrialization . . ., a continuing influx of peoples uprooted and disposed by the Industrial revolution first in Europe and then in Asia" (ibid., 46). The third type was the capital frontier that divided "the would-be exploiters of resources from the possessors of surplus capital" and was mainly concentrated in the cities (ibid.). In each of the three frontiers, "the realm of scarcity was confronting a realm of abundance and stimulated a profitable interchange" (ibid., 45).

By breaking the concept of the frontier into the three "frontiers" (we could think of them as conditions), Slotkin emphasized that, rich as it was, the land, to produce the abundancy it was praised for, required an investment of working hands and capital. The man's relation with the land was not an individual endeavor: it was predefined by the social relation, and the major opposition lay not between the man and the land, but within society; the land, in this layout, was a mediating subject for the two social agencies to collaborate and negotiate on their investment and outcomes. The myth, on the contrary, presented "the sources of wealth as lying outside society, in an unappropriated natural wildness rather than as the product of social labor" (ibid.). In the frontier mythology, land attainment became the only theme, whereas the labor–capital input was obscured and silenced. Nature, with "its abundant and cheap resources," became seen as possessing the value in itself that needed only to be unpacked, and neither the labor nor the capital had anything to do with the creation of that value. Myth made the economic relations in the West look free "of the costs and moral claims put forward by the laboring classes in the Metropolis"; the acquisition of wealth in the West became "an antidote to social conflict" the Metropolis was "contaminated with" (ibid., 41, 45).

There were grounds for such an interpretation, and they nested in significant differences between European and American labor. If in Europe of that time wealth "could be accumulated only by drudgery and self-denial, by intensifying labor to increase the productivity" (Slotkin 1973, 46), American labor was, in fact, the front line of the "colonial conquest" with "exotic and adventurous ways of becoming rich" as an immediate economic reality (ibid.). Accordingly, in frontier mythology, the labor's and the capital's inputs were substituted not only with the abundancy of the land, but also with the entrepreneurs' spirit of a heroic individual.

Slotkin described the process of clearing up the story of Western exploration from the class conflict, and we can argue that such a clearance was a condition for making the story into a nation-building mythology. If embodied into the core of national identity, the class conflict could provide causes for culture wars and civil conflicts and thus had a potential to create a fracture within it. Presenting the frontier as a non-controversial (in economic sense) exploration performed by the individuals not categorized in term of the social classes was likelier to create a sense of national unity and the conditions distinguishable from those of the metropolis.

As Bill Clinton's 1992 campaign's "mantra"—"It's the economy, stupid"—suggested (Pack 2016), despite the clearing of the myth from economic meanings, the economy remained at the heart of the agenda of presidential candidates. Stanley Greenberg (2022) reminded us that the workers had traditionally constituted the Democratic electorate, and that, for instance, the winning presidential campaign of Bill Clinton in 1992, as well as Al Gore's campaign of 2000, which won the popular vote, were working class–oriented. Greenberg also pointed out that Ronald Reagan, in 1984, picked up the votes of "discontented white factory workers across America's Rust Belt" who were "betrayed by Democrats" (Greenberg 2022). (However, some express doubt that the impactful shift of the workers from the Democratic to Republican Party really happened and was not a media-produced manipulation of statistics; see, for instance, Neal Gabler 2016.) The way Reagan talked to the workers was exemplified in his 1981 inaugural address: "We have every right to dream heroic dreams. Those who say that we're in a time when there are not heroes, they just don't know where to look. You can see heroes every day going in and out of factory gates" (Reagan 1981). Although Reagan's economic policies were notoriously harsh on the workers, the narrative that merged the labor with heroic myth proved to be a winning strategy.

Despite that the economy and the frontier themes both remain popular in presidential electoral politics, these two do not merge, and the economic meanings of the frontier remain unclaimed. When the economy becomes a part of presidential electoral discourse, the later focuses mainly on distribution and consumption; taxes, poverty, prices, supply are dominating themes, all about an already earned income. Issues related to production (and distribution as it relates to wages and other compensation for the labor) are rarely given attention other than a mere mention, with the exception of job creation, which is usually presented as a part of the business' development and does not specify the conditions for the labor force. Probably, two 2016 presidential campaigns, that of Bernie Sanders with his working class–oriented agenda and the capital-oriented campaign of Donald Trump were the most noticeable exceptions.

If Reagan brought cinematic fame to politics, Trump supported his presidential ambition with the biography of a developer. His political agenda centered on the economy and precisely on production. Unlike other candidates, who publicly shy away from their wealth and, most importantly, their decision-making power with regard to the economy and finances, Trump presented himself as a capital holder, a decision- and deal maker. He spoke of himself openly in terms of economic interest and openly stood on the side of capital. In theory, that should have alienated the economically disadvantaged blue-collar voters. However, as the 2016 election show, the opposite happened: Trump's agenda appealed precisely to the working class.

The point was that Trump brought the production part of the economy and the capital–labor relations—the essence of capitalism—to the center of the discussion; he recognized the labor as a legitimate participant of the discussion, as a decision maker, and he pulled, at least in the way he spoke of it, the whole socioeconomic setting back to the core relation of classic capitalism. His "below six-grader grammar" (Moyer 2016) was probably not as much a sign of his communicative deficiency or an attempt to appeal to the insufficient education of his electorate (as it was commonly presented by the commentators), as to respond to the need for clarity in assessing the current state of American capitalism, the changing essence of which was hidden from the public by multiplications of political and analytical narratives and their excessive intricacy.

Trump was, essentially, making a deal: "you vote for me, I give you good jobs." Though Trump clearly identified himself as belonging to the opposite class, the appeal of his address was that he spoke to the workers in a language of class interest. He broke the spell, violated the prohibition on the overt capital–labor negotiation, and invited the labor to also define themselves in economic categories. Trump addressed the workers as a collective economic actor, empowered them by returning their collective name to the national discourse, and thus recognized their role as key participants in creating the great American past and future. The working class, the lost actor in the landscape of national pride stigmatized as those who "did not make it," hidden in small towns of the upper Midwest, wiped out from the national mythology, were invited by Trump to reclaim their place in it. The MAGA slogan acquired an elevating meaning of returning to the sacred lands of the frontier as a part of it, moreover, as the agency behind the very fact of its existence. "As unlikely as it may seem, Trump, a billionaire, is the voice of the forgotten American working class" (McDowell 2016).

The land–man relations played the role in crystallization of Trump's electorate and in the way his electorate was portrait by his opponents. "The reservoir of frontier land was to provide a guarantee that each citizen would always have a reasonable chance to acquire land, no matter what the distribution of wealth and power in metropolis might be" (Slotkin 1985, 110); however, by the 1890s, when the closure of the frontier was announced, "the days of limitless free land were over" (Murdoch 2001, 21); so were the equal opportunities based on the availability of free land. Centering the frontier story on the land and ignoring the role of labor in the production of wealth meant that, with the exhaustion of the free land, the opportunities were also depleted. The deprivation of land availability together with the frontier myth providing a conventional model of a story of individual success through the land acquisition show that the "angry" Trump's electorate had historically entrenched reasons to be frustrated. The fact that Trump spoke boldly and angrily appealed to many because it validated their own frustration that was, on the one side, fed by the conditioning mythology and, on the other, suppressed by the constraints of political correctness. Trump's overt expression of anger responded to the quest for public articulation of their own frustration. When the myth re-encountered its economic meanings, and the major value creating agency woke, the man returned to the point of his existential trauma of losing the land, to the moment where the glory of the promise turned into existential deprivation and disorientation. The "gender gap" in Trump's electorate (Sokolove 2020), the most noticeable part of whom were "masculine men" (Thomson-DeVeaux and Conroy 2020) with their reinforced manliness, was, at least in part, predefined by the call of the myth, to which the "angry white men" have a special kinship.

By reestablishing in the frontier story its economic substance, Trump evoked and fulfilled nostalgia for the initial, unchanged, real frontier, that frontier that was more of a reality than of a story. Paradoxically, by doing so, Trump restored the holistic character of the imaginable frontier and opened the room for the myth (and the frontier) to progress again—returning to the frontier's fundamental quality. With opening an opportunity for the further progression of the frontier, the hero also received room to move if not to a higher level, then at least to a different kind of challenge and, with that, to a new level of heroism to perform.

With the re-incorporation of initial economic meanings, the divisive ideology of socioeconomic classes was also brought back, and this had two major consequences. First, the workers reclaimed their place in the frontier myth, which caused a revival of the initial meanings of what it meant to be an American. Second, because they were named in terms of the socioeconomic class, they received a flash of a unifying ideology that, for better or for worse, enabled them to perform as a collective, large-scale social force with a distinctive agency; that agency instantly showed itself through the results of the 2016 elections.

New scapes: cowboy goes metropolitan

While ignoring the input of the labor and centering on the abundancy of the land and individual heroism, myth stripped the cowboy hero of his immediate job responsibilities. When the class issue penetrated the myth, it revealed the class position of the cowboy, who rejoined the labor force and found himself in a struggle not against the land but against the labor market and other socioeconomic forces that set conditions for him. "The cowboy is a hero of an agrarian frontier where everyone can claim a free land. . . . When the frontier is gone, the cowboy myth becomes the urban action myth" (Wright 2001, 23). This change had happened before Donald Trump announced his presidential ambitions, the wave Trump rode had already gained its momentum (in presidential politics as well) and revealed itself to the potential electorate through the popular culture.

In the 1930s, Franklin Roosevelt's New Deal programs "reorganized American politics around urban ethnicity and class," breaking with pastoral tradition and causing "nostalgia for the land" (Rogin 1987, 184). The cinematic art also responded to the tendencies that brought those policies to life, and the 1980 film *Urban Cowboy* presented a new type of a Western man: a landless hardworking fellow, who relocated to the city in a hope for job and had to readjust to a new, technologized, and urbanized environment. The idea contained clear symbolic underlining of the Western hero "relocating" to the new grounds. Without the land available for the hero to acquire, he found himself back to the capital–labor relations from which the abundancy of the "virgin" lands promised an escape. Because the capital–labor relations were not a part of the American myth, by entering into them the hero entered the area of his existential deprivation. The inconsistency of the mythological charge of the cowboy and the sobering reality of him turning from the hero into a labor pool unit constituted the *Urban Cowboy* drama.

If the agrarian space "liberated the white man from social conflict" (Wright 2001, 181), the cityscape "liberated" the man from the agrarian space and threw him into the wilderness of the city. It was the city, not the country, that provided "the primary context for the modern-day western heroes and villains" (Rushing 1983, 15). The myth, having started against the background of the frontier wilderness, then moving to the agrarian pastoral, then to the town and, eventually, to an urbanized area, was now set against the metropolis cityscape.

The setting of *Urban Cowboy* was transitional, preserving—typically for myth—an opposition: it was the city of Houston, a giant metropolitan area, yet a part of Texas, a traditional cowboy land. The protagonist found the Houston area divided into two zones—one with electrical lightning, a prosperous congestion of skyscrapers, and another with a gloomy set of trailers, a job-defined schedule, and cheap entertainment. The two girls of the Western classic myth received an updated placement in the *Urban Cowboy*, one girl belonging to the prosperous cityscape set and the other struggling at the margins of the metropolis and poverty. The movie offered no clear indication of which of the two girls was good and which was bad; the two-girls dilemma that served as a clear moral marker in the initial layout of the myth was erased in the movie, and the hero faced a new challenge of having to decide the moral dilemma by himself. It moved the hero further toward his inner complexity and psychologization. The "urban cowboy" had a choice between the two worlds, two scapes of Texan metropolis, two girls; the class conflict had already been revealed to him, and he refused the temptations of the city and chose, not without a drama and frustration, the modesty of the one-story, obedient to the factory horn realm of the working man.

The transformation of the hero articulated in *Urban Cowboy*, already one step toward the debunking of myth, yet opened an opportunity for the myth to continue; it presented one more trope to explore: the cowboy returning to the relations fused with class conflict, but this time on the side of the capital; the cowboy, choosing the skyscrapered city. Trump exploited precisely this opportunity, impersonating the turn of the urban cowboy into cowboy metropolitan, who managed to get on top of the economic hierarchy, on the top levels of a luxury skyscraper—a cowboy who made it.

As the myth was progressing through the new scapes and oppositions, Donald Trump was moving in his career in a pace and by the trajectory to where they would, eventually, intersect. The logic of myth was unfolding toward the point where a character like Trump could fit the emerging niche in the new format of the frontier mythology. Michael Ryan and Douglas Kellner (1988) defined the 1970s and the beginning of the 1980s—the time when Trump entered business—as the hero revival films era; the cowboy-hero had undergone radical transformation; he now rode an electrical bull and obeyed the factory horn (Ryan and Kellner 1988). In 1978, when the first *Star Wars* episode hit the cinema, Trump "launched his family's first Manhattan venture, the renovation of the derelict Commodore Hotel" (NBC News 2016); in the following four years, the other two episodes of the original trilogy were made, and the Trump Tower in Manhattan was built. The 1980s, the years of Reagan's presidency, "the era of the urban cowboy" (Rushing 1983, 14), were the years of the revival of cowboy aesthetics and the re-emergence of the American Western Myth (ibid.); in 1987, when "the era of the hero was over" (Ryan and Kellner 1988, 297), Trump registered as a Republican, and in the late 1980s, he began transitioning into a TV personality, made cameo appearances, and became a member of the Screen Actors Guild. Those are seemingly irrelevant parallels, but the progression of Trump's becoming who he came as to the election day (or at least the way that progression was presented by the media) was in line with how a success was envisioned in a collective imagination of those people, who would have to throw the ballots—a collective imagination, charged by the televised frontier mythology. Just as Roosevelt

Donald Trump 53

created the myth which he saddled during his presidential campaign, Trump rode a visualized mythology that promoted the criteria of success by which he was judged.

With Trump breaking into the frontier mythology, the setting moved yet further from the West to the East, both geographically and symbolically. The frontier settled in the heart of urbanism—New York City—and in the heart of New York City, Manhattan, a minutes-long walk from the Time Square, on the top floors of Trump Tower. The horizontal agricultural landscape and a life that was nature-paced, structured by traditions and work routine, turned into hectic, sleepless rounds under electric lights. The disregard for natural rhythms, the abundancy and artificiality that supplanted ascetism and naturalness—Trump and the whole entourage were in opposition to the classic cowboy hero and his environment. At the same time, the new setting was, in a way, more genuine, more natural in the context of the progressed myth, defined by its developmental logic and not by the outdated imagery.

Trump's business record as a developer, by definition engaged with the land, became a helpful detail in infusing his mythological placement. The cowboy hero had already gone urban, so Trump's attachment to Manhattan, the embodiment of urbanism at the heights of technological advancements, were pertinent. In Trump's version, the cowboy found the land in its new location, in its new quality, and figured out a new way of relating to it. Moreover, he turned the land into a technology-induced "garden" and fought new "villains"—which he identified as unprofessional and corrupt city officials and politicians. He moved the "frontier line" of his family business beyond that established by his father, both geographically—to Manhattan, the national and global business epicenter—and socially, targeting the wealthiest consumers nationwide and globally. References to the land–man relations were sometimes direct, as Trump and the land were a common motive in his video imagery. Either he was flying a helicopter over the mighty Manhattan, gazing at Central Park sprawled wide underneath, or he was walking his golf courses—his interest, his investment, his glance were fixed on land. A 2016 NBC documentary (NBC News 2016) pictured Trump standing on the bridge, looking at an undeveloped piece of land on Manhattan's West Side; he had purchased that land long ago and was, since, keeping it as an inspiring potential—a "wild" land before him, "a magic locus of potential wealth" (Slotkin 1985, 39). The places he was involved in developing were among the most expensive in the country—Manhattan, the Florida sea line, an array of Las Vegas casinos—a presumable source of enrichment, a promise of prosperity. This very engagement was important, regardless of whether it was successful. Thus, the mentioning of the bankruptcies Trump's business had gone through had to be, supposedly, harmful for his presidential ambitions, but the affair with the land glimmering from underneath the bankruptcy was what the real, hidden tale was about; the affair with the land and the entrepreneurs spirit constituted, probably, not a less captivating story than some stories of success. After all, the original frontier man's affair with the land was not short of drama either.

In Trump's story, not by any means limited by his reputation as a developer, this developer's part has mostly been emphasized. The media show him doing business on land, building on it, fixing someone's poor management of it (such as in a case with the Wollman Ring), erecting towers with his name on them—constantly staying in a turbulent but stable relationship with the land, almost married to it. His affairs with women, verbal or physical, gross or doting, were of a lesser scale than his enduring relations with the land. His image of a developer won over his image of a playboy and a husband, no matter how difficult those relations were. That was his fight, his trial, his challenge, from which he rose (or was presented so) as the winner. Trump returned the land from the faraway galaxies to Earth, materialized it back from its mental presentations, disenchanted its resistance; he burned the frog skin of its mythic incarnation. If Roosevelt witnessed the exhauster of the free available land, if Reagan explored, exploited, and expropriated the representations of the land in the fantasy world, Trump rediscovered the opportunities for its exploration on the earthly ground. Under Reagan, the land as a challenge was gone to other planets and outer space, as well as to foreign countries (such as the "Evil Empire" of the USSR), both remote and alien. Trump, on the contrary, rediscovered the opportunities for the man–land relation on the American soil and found a way to present himself as a wild, outright, uncivilized manly man—a striking contrast to a conventional politician on the stage of the national presidential debate.

Trump eased the demands for a good-all-around hero and reopened the room for exhibiting morally ambiguous actions and connections, as a MAGA hat replacement of the white Stetson indicated. An important aspect of going back to the initial variations of the frontier hero was that the restored initial meanings included those related to morals, precisely, the moral ambiguity and the outlaw features. Acceptance of this part of the "hero journey" (borrowing Campbell's term) opened the Overton window toward acceptance by the public of behaviors deviating from the moral standards established in presidential politics, as long as those behaviors were authentic to the hero. Trump came to politics with a record of controversies, but placement of his presidential image within the logic of myth turned the ambiguity into a proof of authenticity inherent to an unabridged version of the frontier hero.

Myth continued

With all the dramatic developments that the frontier myth encountered throughout the century, from its first articulation by Theodore Roosevelt to its tacit restoration by Donald Trump, a major development occurred in the hero himself. The frontier as a spatial concept was exhausted, and further progression could only occur within the hero, in the microcosm of his inner world. Initially a simple, generic, action-driven performer, fixed in oppositions and possessing very little, if at all, complexity, the hero, eventually, obtained psychological sophistication and grew up into a more elaborated, nuanced character.

This complexity, again, could not remain within the hero; it had to be externalized—again—as any other opposition the myth presented and the hero encountered. Therefore, the inner complexity, the inner opposition, the inner fight had to be, yet again, externalized and impersonated. The hero's inner contradiction, having grown in tension to the limits, broke into two major opposing entities, into two personalities, each embodying one of the opposite sets of traits. One character—the hero—was thought to embody all the good, and the other—his opponent—was to embody all the evil. The danger possessed by the evil antihero and the responsibility of the hero to defeat him became the task to take on to prove the heroic status.

In the national political discourse (given that the discourse was not thought to be divisive), the antihero, the embodiment of an absolute evil, could only be either a foreigner or an alien. Geographically foreign, socially alien, politically perverted, morally insufficient—a true villain, a nearly perfect villain—came on time.

References

Gabler, Neal. 2016. "The Media Myth of the Working-Class Reagan Democrats." *Moyers*, May 6. https://billmoyers.com/story/media-myth-working-class-reagan-democrats/.

Greenberg, Stanley. 2022. "Democrats, Speak to Working-Class Discontent." *The American Prospect*, February 14. https://prospect.org/politics/democrats-speak-to-working-class-discontent/.

McDowell, Christopher R. 2016. "Trump Is Voice of Forgotten Working Class." *Cincinnati, The Enquirer*, September 23. www.cincinnati.com/story/opinion/contributors/2016/09/23/trump-voice-forgotten-working-class/90835476/.

Moyer, Justin. 2016. "Trump's Grammar in Speeches 'Just Below 6th Grade Level,' Study Finds." *The Washington Post*, March 18.

Murdoch, David H. 2001. *The American West: The Invention of Myth*. Cardiff: Welsh Academic Press.

NBC News. 2016. "1980s: How Donald Trump Created Donald Trump." *NBC News*, Filmed video 4:51, July. www.youtube.com/watch?v=_FLo14GMYos.

Pack, Mark. 2016. "The War Room: How Clinton Won in 92—and the Importance of Thanking Helpers." November 5. www.markpack.org.uk/39790/the-war-room-how-clinton-won-in-92-and-the-importance-of-thanking-helpers/.

Reagan, Ronald. 1981. "Inaugural Address." Reagan Library, January 20. www.reaganlibrary.gov/archives/speech/inaugural-address-1981.

Rogin, Michael P. 1987. *Ronald Reagan the Movie: And Other Episodes of Political Demonology*. Berkeley, Los Angeles and London: University of California Press.

Rushing, Janice Hocker. 1983. "The Rhetoric of the American Western Myth." *Communication Monographs* 50 (1): 14–32. doi:10.1080/03637758309390151.

Ryan, Michael, and Douglas Kellner. 1988. *Camera Politica: The Politics and Ideology of Contemporary Hollywood Film*. Bloomington: Indiana University Press.

Slotkin, Richard. 1973. *Regeneration Through Violence: The Mythology of the American Frontier, 1600–1860*. Middleton: Wesleyan University Press.

———. 1981. "Nostalgia and Progress: Theodore Roosevelt's Myth of the Frontier." *American Quarterly* 33 (5): 608–37. www.ezproxy.shsu.edu/10.2307/2712805.

———. 1985. *The Fatal Environment: The Myth of the Frontier in the Age of Industrialization, 1800–1890*. New York: Atheneum.

———. 1992. *Gunfighter Nation: Myth of the Frontier in Twentieth Century America*. New York: Atheneum.

Sokolove, Michael. 2020. "Why Does Trump Win with White Men?" *New York Times*, October 3. www.nytimes.com/2020/10/23/opinion/sunday/gender-gap-2020-election.html.

Thomson-DeVeaux, Amelia, and Meredith Conroy. 2020. "Why so Many Men Stuck with Trump in 2020." *Five Thirty-Eight*, December 9. https://fivethirtyeight.com/features/why-so-many-men-stuck-with-trump-in-2020/.

Wright, Will. 2001. *The Wild West: The Mythical Cowboy and Social Theory*. London: Southern Oaks and New Delhi: Sage Publication.

5 Vladimir Putin

"Stolen" meanings of the frontier and a supplementing hero

Here comes the villain

If Donald Trump made a surprising arrival into the gallery of the frontier hero characters, the presence of the Russian president in it is beyond remarkable. Nevertheless, Putin joined the club. He entered American presidential mythology in two ways: as the villain—an impersonalized opposition to all the good and to the hero personally—and as an embodiment of some of the classic attributes of the frontierer, lacking in the image of Trump.

The law of the genre: "make the villain first" seems to be fully applicable to the layout of the characters in the frontier myth. Like the land was primary in opposition to the man and evoked a heroic response from him, now, at the new level of the myth, it is a villain who presents the challenge, making his presence in the drama an absolute necessity.

Peter Homans (1961), in his analysis of the Western movie genre, observed a consistent pattern in the behavior of the cowboy in a bar before and after his villainous opponent enters the stage. "Contrived indolence," "apparent laxity," "nothing directional or purposeful about him," "lax to the point of laziness," "somewhat bored"—the hero is just hanging around. With the entrance of the villain, though, the hero changes instantly and radically: "gone are the indolence, laxity, and lack of intention. Now he is infused with vitality, direction, and seriousness" (ibid., 79).

The entrance of the villain revitalizes not only the hero but the community he represents. Here is how Homans described the effect of the villain upon the town:

> The impact of this evil one on the town is electric, as though a switch had been thrown, suddenly animating its vitality, purpose, and direction. Indeed, it is evil, rather than good, which actually gives meaning to the lives. . . . The townsfolk now share a new identity. . . . United by a common threat, the town loses its desolate, aimless quality. It becomes busy.
>
> (ibid.)

Thus, it came in handy that the absolute political villain preceded the hero. By the time Trump took office, Putin had long been an established politician, almost eternal, so from the time standpoint, he provided a solid opportunity to make him a benchmark for the journey of the hero-in-becoming.

The role given to Putin might or might not coincide with his real qualities and moral stands; he might be as bad as he is told to be, or he might be a lesser evil; the truthfulness of his presentation in the media is not of any significance to myth. The presence of a villain is important as the point of reference for telling the good from the bad, and for the reassurance of an absolute moral authority of the hero.

After the frontier extended and dissolved, in Reagan's execution of the myth, the very figure of a villain became a new frontier, serving as the initiation agency, a pass to a big politics. A demonized figure of Putin in this role made him an indispensable figure in current American mythology. In the way the wilderness of the virgin land used to define the character of the frontierer, nowadays, defeating Putin, even just in a speech, presumably, makes a politician into a hero. The bigger the evil, the more grandiose is the victory over him, so there should be no limit to the badness of the evil impersonator. Presented as an embodiment of all the evil on earth and beyond, bad as and beyond one can be, Putin has been made into a figure of grandiose power, an absolute evil, a carrier of all the ills and deviations, moral and psychological.

The part of the villain in American political mythology is so important that Putin is, probably, going to remain in the cast even after he retires from politics. After the ultimate demonization Putin was granted in the Western media, there is no room for an "improvement," no chance to outgrow his villainy; there is no place for a bigger villain, or even for a villain of an equal scale. The stakes have been raised to the limits, and from that height, the only way can be downward, through downscaling the villainy of the antagonist. The problem is that downscaling the major villain would defeat the purpose of constricting him as a part of mythological layout.

How is that problem going to be resolved? We might learn about it in the near future. One way of maintaining the intensity of the mythological plot after Putin retires from the role would be moving the divisive line from international politics to within the national borders and casting for the role of the major villain a local, national personae, who is either playing, or is said to be playing a leading role in an acute culture war. This strategy could, probably, provide at least some leverage for maintaining the scale of the stakes; it could be fraught, however, with the destruction of national unity and crisis in national identity, potentially endangering the very existence of the "one nation, indivisible."

"Is he one of us?"

The frontier drama, moved to within the industrial and then postindustrial landscapes, and the hero, who departed as far from the original cowboy as at all possible, made him, through the chain of the transformations, lose some of his initial traits, precisely those that were such a big part of the myth and its cinematic representation at the first place. A contradictory situation occurred. On the one hand, the modification of the myth as presented by Donald Trump opened a new path for the myth to continue and for the renovated image of the hero to become more adequate to the transformed settings—a hero wearing the cowboy boots and hat would be too exotic in the electric lights of Manhattan. On the other hand, the innovative scenery and radically altered cowboyhood of this later modification was accompanied with vanishing some of the classic traits of the hero, such as his closeness to the wilderness, his reserved manners, asceticism, his loneliness and unrootedness. Without those solidly established traits, the cowboy image is doomed to lose much of its primary authenticity and attraction, its nostalgic appeal.

A solution to this contradiction would be to allocate the missing traits to an auxiliary character. It would probably be better if such a character came from domestic politics, but the figure would have to be of an equal—presidential—scale, and there obviously, can be only one American president at a time. Also, if the man were to be of an equal scale to an absolutely empowered hero, he could only be a villain, an existential rival; otherwise, if that character was on the side of the good, he could not measure up to the hero; he could only be of a smaller scale. Both requirements pointed to a foreign leader; either himself or his country would present a challenge serious enough for the hero to respond to with all his might.

It happened so that Putin (rather his media portrayal) met both criteria. In addition to being a perfect representation of the villain, his media image also carried a collection of classic Western traits, precisely those missing in the image of Trump. If Trump's image was allied with the progressing logic of the myth, the image of Putin turned out to be more in line with the classic, nostalgic portrayal of the frontier man. When the American frontier hero reincarnated into his upgraded Trump version, the media-Putin showed as the American tough close to his classic format, feeding to the nostalgia for the original image. In this regard, Patrick Buchanan's memorable sentiment, "Is Putin one of us?" (Buchanan 2013) takes on new meanings.

Good physical shape and involvement in outdoor activities—not the strongest side of Trump's image—have been a significant part of the promoted image of Putin. He is typically shown in a manner that equated his physical condition with toughness—the horseback riding topless in Siberia is not, indeed, for the weak, if only because of the harsh Siberian mosquitoes and the cold. The deliberately ostentatious wealth of Trump's palaces and his lifestyle arrangements are overall in contrast with Putin's emphasized modesty; his reportedly enormous wealth has never been on display. In the splendid premises of the Kremlin and other grand locations in which Putin is habitually shown, he looks deliberately humble and ascetic. Trump's involvement with women, in and outside of marriages, have been widely discussed in the press and by Trump himself, whereas Putin's personal life remains an absolute taboo for any kind of public discussion, except for his terminated marriage, about which he and his wife of over 30 years themselves publicly announced on camera. After divorce, he was rumored to be married again, but that was not officially confirmed. If the public is aware of the locations, exteriors, and interiors of Trump's homes, Putin's locations are not disclosed; the public does not know where he sleeps, where he lives, where he is retreating after leaving his office. In these contrasting presentations of the two men, Putin is more resemblant of the classic cowboy, the Marlboro man type, emotionally disconnected, lonely, rough, ascetic, serving his people and retreating "into the sunset." In contrast to Trump with his highly controversial communication style and expressive gesturing (see: Sclafani 2018), Putin is typically shown as emotionally reserved and poker-faced, his gestures are extremely scarce, and his speech is precise and laconic. In the media, he is called "soft-spoken," an "iron hand" man, reminiscent of the "Dakota Territory rancher and former Rough Rider Teddy Roosevelt . . . who kicked off the notion of presidential 'cowboy diplomacy' by summarizing his approach to his international policy as, 'Speak softly and carry a big stick'" (Bonner 2008).

Thus, the correlation of the major (Trump) and supplemental (Putin) heroes took astonishing turns with a bizarre, whimsical intertwining of the elements of classic and renovated images, their symbolisms, and variations of meanings playing against various contexts. Trump and Putin together produced, at the will of the media, a joint incarnation of the frontier hero, a quirky weave of the villainy and heroic merits, a combination of an upgraded post-industrial cowboy that did not look like himself, and an outdated but nostalgically missed classic image that, on closer inspection, turned out to belong to an alien figure.

References

Bonner, Lucky. 2008. "The Last Cowboy President? How U.S. Presidents Have Re-Created Themselves as Cowboys since the Turn of the 20th Century." *True West*, May 1. https://truewestmagazine.com/article/the-last-cowboy-president/.
Buchanan, Patrick. 2013. "Is Putin One of Us?" *Patrick J. Buchannan—Official Website*, December 17. https://buchanan.org/blog/putin-one-us-6071.
Homans, Peter. 1961. "Puritanism Revisited: An Analysis of the Contemporary Screen-Image Western." *Studies in Public Communication* 3: 73–84.
Sclafani, Jennifer. 2018. *Talking Donald Trump: A Sociolinguistic Study of Style, Metadiscourse, and Political Identity*. London and New York: Routledge.

Concluding thoughts

Three major conclusions can be drawn from the logic of myth as it has been constructed through presidential politics. The first conclusion is related to the making of the presidential image of Trump, the second is related to the frontier myth itself and its potency to serve as the nation-building construct, and the third is related to the situation, when the nation's mythology runs into its logical exhauster.

Built into the architecture of American frontier mythology, the presidential image of Trump is unsinkable, at least for as long as it remains within the myth, and for as long as the myth itself holds its stance. The myth-infused image is immune against the attacks by Trump's political opponents, against the attempts to destroy it or lessen its attractiveness to the part of the electorate, with whom that image clicked in the first place. Compromising evidence or accusations in moral or legal ambiguity cannot significantly harm the image built into the structure of myth because this kind of image resists the judgment based on the principles of law and ethics. Such immunity comes from the quality of myth to legitimate any practice or feature that is normalized within the myth, regardless of how that practice or feature is characterized outside of the myth's reach. Although myth provides a place for the showdown of the good and the bad, the characters enacting that showdown acquire moral attributes only after the myth converts into an ideological statement. The good and the bad are not attributions of myth per se, because myth is precisely a story of their becoming. It is a story of condensing heroic actions and the obstacles that come from other characters and forces into the opposites, for which moral categories become markers afterwards. Moral stand is a result, not the cause of the confrontation; or, rather the stand in a confrontation acquires characteristics of morality afterwards. The mythic rivals, who become perceived as good and bad, both have an equally existential necessity to act the way they do; the very sense of those two opposite characters is to perform the forces that create and sustain the world and infuse it with vitality. Inapplicability of moral categories to assessing doings and words of a politician, whose image is aligned with the myth, can be demonstrated by Trump's boast at his 2016 rally in Iowa: "The polls say I have the most loyal people. . . . I could stand in the middle of Fifth Avenue and shoot somebody, and I would not lose any voters" (Diamond 2016).

Because the hero's actions, regardless of the judgment, are of an existential value, the features of the hero, including those marked as negative, are also validated. Cleared by the logic of myth, those features contribute to the sustainability of the myth's structure, which is not complete without that element, and it is not as much an ethical or legal mode of that feature, but the very presence of it that becomes important. Whatever the feature is, it is going to be marked within the myth as natural and normal, even if it contradicts the established moral principles and political conformity of society in which the myth operates. Every element of myth structure presents itself as natural and necessary, regardless of whether it complies with the standards of morality and the logic of critical reasoning and whether it sustains the fact check. If an image of a politician is built into the national myth, it is not the morals and established rules that serve as a measure of the politician's doings, but, conversely, his doings become a new norm in doing politics. The criteria of truthfulness and appropriateness of a message or a whole shared mental pattern peculiar to the myth miss the target; those belong to the arsenal of an information war, while myth, when in war or a competition, belongs to the cognitive sphere. Echoing Claude Levi-Strauss, who insisted that "a myth can be translated only by another myth" (Doniger 1995, x), we can say that a myth can only be defeated by its own means.

No rational arguments, no fact check can turn Trump's electorate away from him, for his attractiveness lies within the myth, not within the rational. The only two ways to destroy this enchanting power would be either to strip Trump's political image of its mythical format or shed the myth of its exclusive functions. There are several ways of doing so, from removing the villain as a sparring actor on the political stage—that would mean abandoning Putin as a major theme in American politics—to incorporating the production- and labor-related economic meanings into a national political narrative outside of myth as overtly as Donald Trump did it within the myth.

By bringing up the Russian collusion and otherwise referencing to Putin while talking about Trump, Trump's opponents do the opposite of what they would have to do to defeat him, at least in the realm of political imagery. Associations with Putin do not hurt Trump because the proximity of these two images, no matter whether real or made up by the media, revoke the theme of their heroic duality and embrace the myth structure, which, in turn, solidifies Trump's image. The way to reduce the mythological effect of Trump's image would be discontinuing his imagery from that of Putin, removing the villain from the picture, who, by his very presence, provides the hero with a chance to maintain the heroic status. Removing mythological framing from the narrative could destroy the binary structure of Trump's image, and that is when it could become vulnerable to rational arguments, ethics, and the fact-check.

Another misstep Trump's opponents make is utilizing the Putin-the-Villain theme to bust up their own images. Despite the popularity of this expedient, its effectiveness does not extend to other politicians. It is because Putin-the-Villain is not a substantive figure in American political mythology; he is an auxiliary character to the hero, and it happened so that the role of the hero was allocated to Trump. Hilary Clinton was particularly prolific in mentioning Putin in her speeches, but it did not seem to serve her well—she was not at the right place in the myth. By mentioning Putin as a reference point for contrasting goodness versus badness, Hilary Clinton, or President Biden, or other politicians presenting themselves (or being presented) in dramatic opposition to Putin, can still capitalize on it, but this capitalization will remain an ideological, artificial trick, not nearly as effective as the vivid, mythic Trump–Putin duo.

After the logic of myth was completed and after the myth was revitalized by reclaiming some of the original meanings of the frontier, where can the myth go next? What format of the hero and what structure-forming oppositions can keep it alive and going?

One possible direction would be to continue with incorporating the initial meanings of the reality of the frontier into its mythologized story, such as diversifying the racial and ethnic background of the cowboys, far not all of whom were white, but many were Indigenous, Black, or Hispanic. Another way of extending the myth would be incorporating gender into the story of the frontier, and the feminist literature has already been exploring this opportunity with a prolific and enthralling body of texts. Yet another way to proceed would be to re-emphasize the role of family during the westward expansion. There are other, probably more subtle nuances of the lost meanings of the frontier that could be re-incorporated into a story and prolongate the life of myth by giving it a new developmental impulse.

This way of prolonging the vividness of the myth has natural limitations, though. When myth opens to incorporating all the multiple meaning initially dropped from the story, the added content can, at some point, overgrow the formative capacity of myth and soften its rigid structure. First, an added component might be resistant to conditioning into a structural unit of the myth, resistant to subduing its complexity and variability to the strict logic and reductionist impact of mythologization. Second, myth benefits from the truthfulness of the story to a certain extent only; the story must have enough plasticity in it to not be resistant to distortions of its meanings. For this matter, the story must have the potential to depart from the truth, especially at the moment when the truth can cause the erosion of the structure of myth. There is a danger that when the frontier mythology absorbs all the characters, characteristics, and meanings of the frontier that were dropped off in its classic format, the resulting intellectual product will be historically truthful, but it will not be myth anymore.

This brings us to the question of whether we need the myth at all. Why not replace it with the truthfully told story, inclusive of all the types, who participated in the reality of what the story was supposed to be told about? It is, probably, one of the most fundamental questions to address in current political discussions about national unity. If the "open and ever-expanding frontier" is still "central to American identity" (Grandin 2019), then the vanishing of the frontier myth can put the American identity into crisis until or unless some new, more developmentally appropriate basis for it is found or created. Finding or constructing a new ground for American identity is not an impossible task, and it could happen that the revision of the foundations of national unity will be requested by new actors in politics in the nearest future. Uniformed national identity creates the nation, and the absence or deficiency of the uniting national mythology is likely to contribute to culture wars and social instability.

With the completion of the cowboy's hero journey, the frontier myth exhausted means for its productive use in politics and nation building. All the aspects and the potential resources of the frontier myth, inner and outer, were mobilized, and the mythology outgrew itself. Although the need for myth as a uniting force might be as important as ever, the potency of the frontier myth is in decline. It is not completely faded—yet—as the carrying structure of national consciousness, but it is becoming increasingly irrelevant to the national ideology splintering into many. What is going to replace the frontier myth, and what will become the carrying structural force of the ever-continuing nation building and national unity? This question should be considered before the myth completely melts away.

References

Diamond, Jeremy. 2016. "Trump: I Could Shoot Somebody and Not Lose Voters." *CNN*, January 24. www.cnn.com/2016/01/23/politics/donald-trump-shoot-somebody-support.

Doniger, Wendy. 1995. "Foreword." In *Myth and Meaning: Cracking the Code of Culture*, edited by Claude Levi-Strauss. New York: Schocken Books.

Grandin, Greg. 2019. *The End of the Myth: From the Frontier to the Border Wall in the Mind of America*. New York: Metropolitan Books.

Index

American Dream 25
American Historical Association (AHA) 14–15
antihero 55
audience 6, 18, 36

bandanas 41
Biden, Joe 2; on Xi Jingping 3
body politic 39
Bolton, John 2
border dramas 13
boundary confusion 16, 37–39
Buffalo Bill Cody 13–15, 37
buffalo hunters 22–23
Bush, George W. 8
Bush, Jeb 3

California 17
capital frontier 47
capitalism 49
Cattle Queen of Montana 40–41
China 2
Christianity 40
Clinton, Bill 2, 36, 48, 63
Clinton, Hillary 4
Cody, Bill 13
Cold War 44; *see also* Russia
community 27–29
contradictions 16–21, 28, 31
Cooper, James Fenimore 25
cowboy 11–12, 22–25, 29, 40; metropolitan 51–54; urban 51–52
Crockett, Davy 15–16
Custer, George Armstrong 37

dime novels 12–13, 22, 26

economics 46–49
Eisenhower, Dwight 41
Elizabeth I, Queen 31–32
emasculation 6
evil 55; *see also* villain

family 63
femininity 30–33
films 36–43
frontier: contradiction of myth and 16–20; girl and 30–33; land and the man 20–26; staging the myth and 11–16; towners and 26–29
Frontier Thesis 14
frontierer 7
frontiers 46–47

Geronimo 14
girl, bad 30–32, 51–52
girl, good 30–32, 51–52
Gore, Al 48

Harrison, William Harry 11
hero 7, 19–21, 24, 26–32, 42–44; *see also* cowboy; hunter; soldier
hero's journey 27, 43, 54, 64
Hollywood 35; *see also* Westerns
hunter 14, 23–24

individualism 8, 26, 27, 29

Jeffersonian Garden 20
Johnson, Lyndon 8
journey 27, 43, 54, 64

Index

Kasowitz, Marc 2
king's two bodies 39–40

labor 49–50
labor frontier 47
land 20–26, 42–43, 47, 50; man and 20–26; virgin 16
Levi-Strauss, Claude 62

Madison, James 41
MAGA hat 36, 51
Manhattan 53
masculine politics 5–9
masculinity 5–8, 30, 33, 50; *see also* tough guy
morality 26–27, 61

national identity 18–20
national mythology 6, 25, 49, 64
Native Americans 23
New Deal 51
New York City 53
Nixon, Richard 2, 6

opposition 18–19, 43, 53–54, 57, 63
Oregon 17

paintings 12
Paulding, Kirke 15
persistence 6
physicality 59–60
plays 13
psychologization 29, 52
Putin, Vladimir 57–60, 62–63; toughness and 1, 3–5; *see also* Russia

Reagan, Nancy 38
Reagan, Ronald 6, 8, 35–44, 46, 54
resources frontier 47
Romney, Mitt 6
Roosevelt, Franklin 51
Roosevelt, Theodore 8–9, 37, 54, 60; contradiction of myth and 16–20; gendered opposition and 30–33; land and the man 20–26; performative frontier and 11–16; towners and 26–29

Rough Riders 14
Russia 4–5, 62; *see also* Putin, Vladimir
Russian collusion 62

Sanders, Bernie 49
sectional character 21
Slotkin, Richard 24–25, 39, 46–47
social class 24–26, 48–52
Sons of the Border, The: Sketches of the Life and People on the Far Frontier 20, 26
Soldier 22–25
sovereign 42
Star Wars 43
Stetson 35, 54
Steele, James, W. 20, 26

tough guy 1–9, 27–28
towners 26–29
truth 58, 63
Turner, Frederick 14, 17

upward mobility 25, 40
Urban Cowboy 51–52

Van Buren, William 11
villain 44, 55, 57–60; *see also* Putin, Vladimir
virgin land 16, 23
Virginian, The 13
virginity 31–32

Washington, DC 42
Westerns 6–7, 38–41; villain and 57
Whigs 11
White House 38–39
Wild West Show 13–14
wildness 28
Wister, Owen 13
women 30–33, 51–52, 59–60
working class 50
World's Columbian Exposition (Chicago World Fair) 14–15
Wyoming 13, 32

Xi Jingping 3

For Product Safety Concerns and Information please contact our EU representative GPSR@taylorandfrancis.com
Taylor & Francis Verlag GmbH, Kaufingerstraße 24, 80331 München, Germany

www.ingramcontent.com/pod-product-compliance
Lightning Source LLC
Chambersburg PA
CBHW071823230426
43670CB00013B/2553